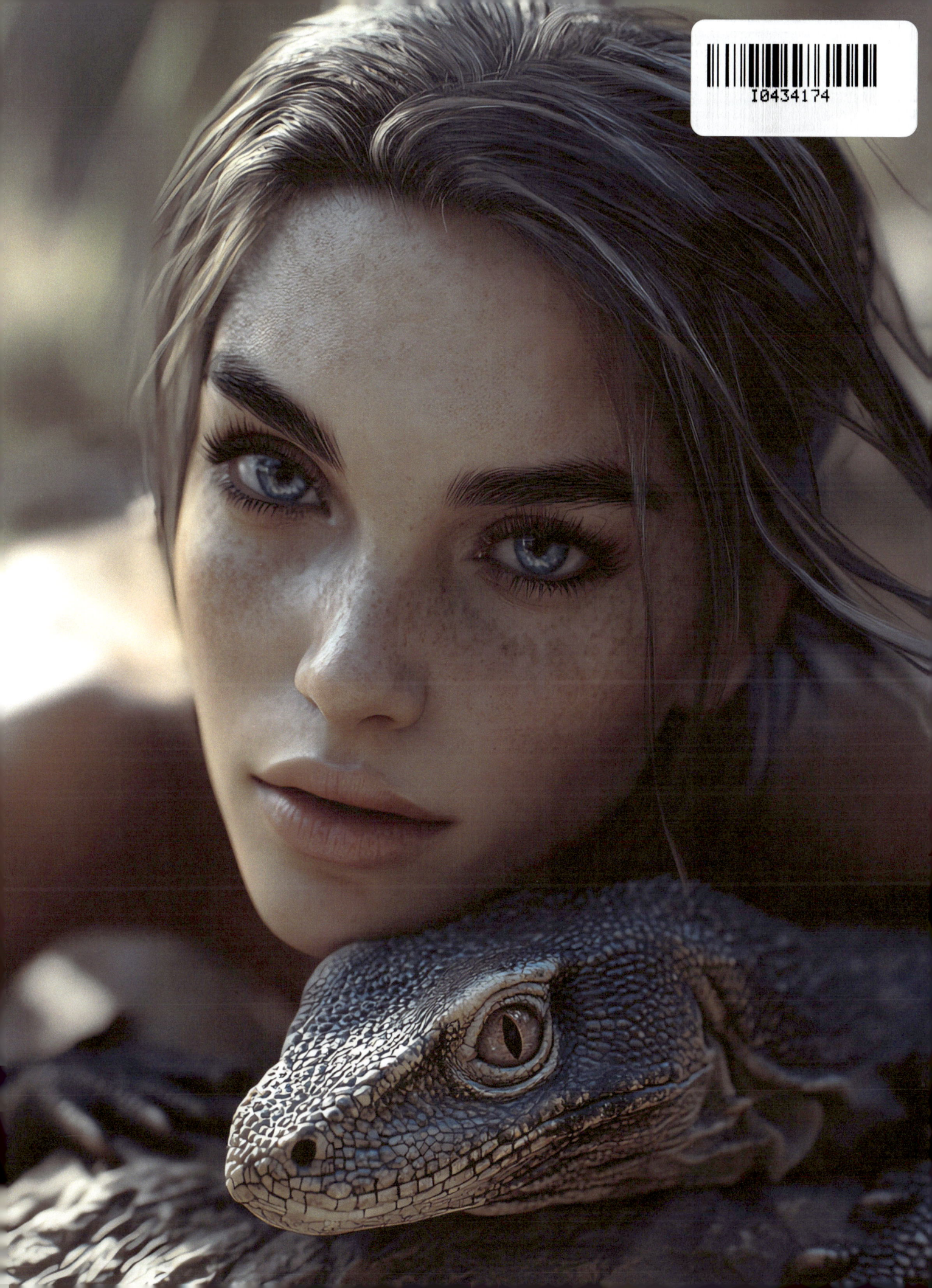

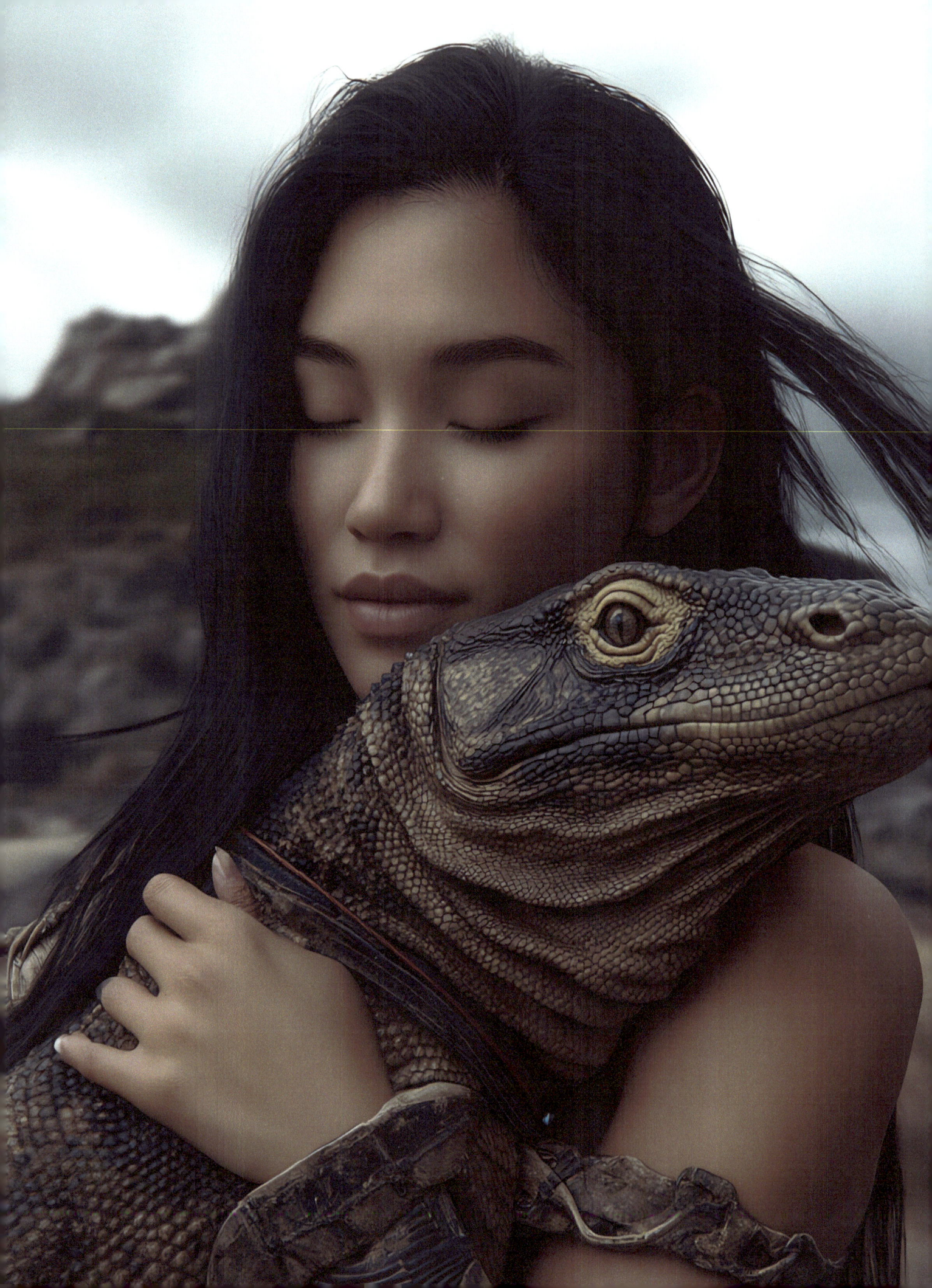

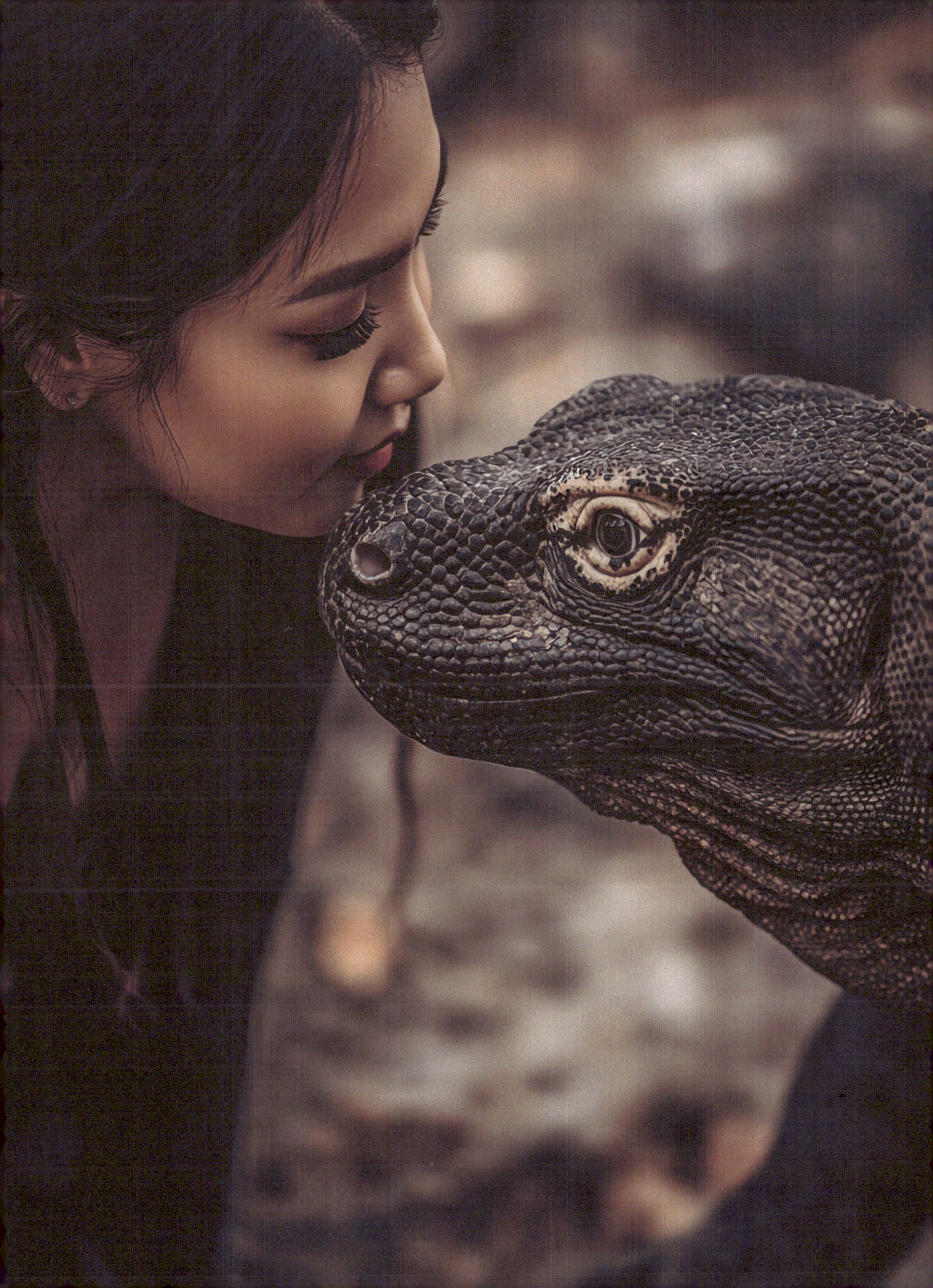

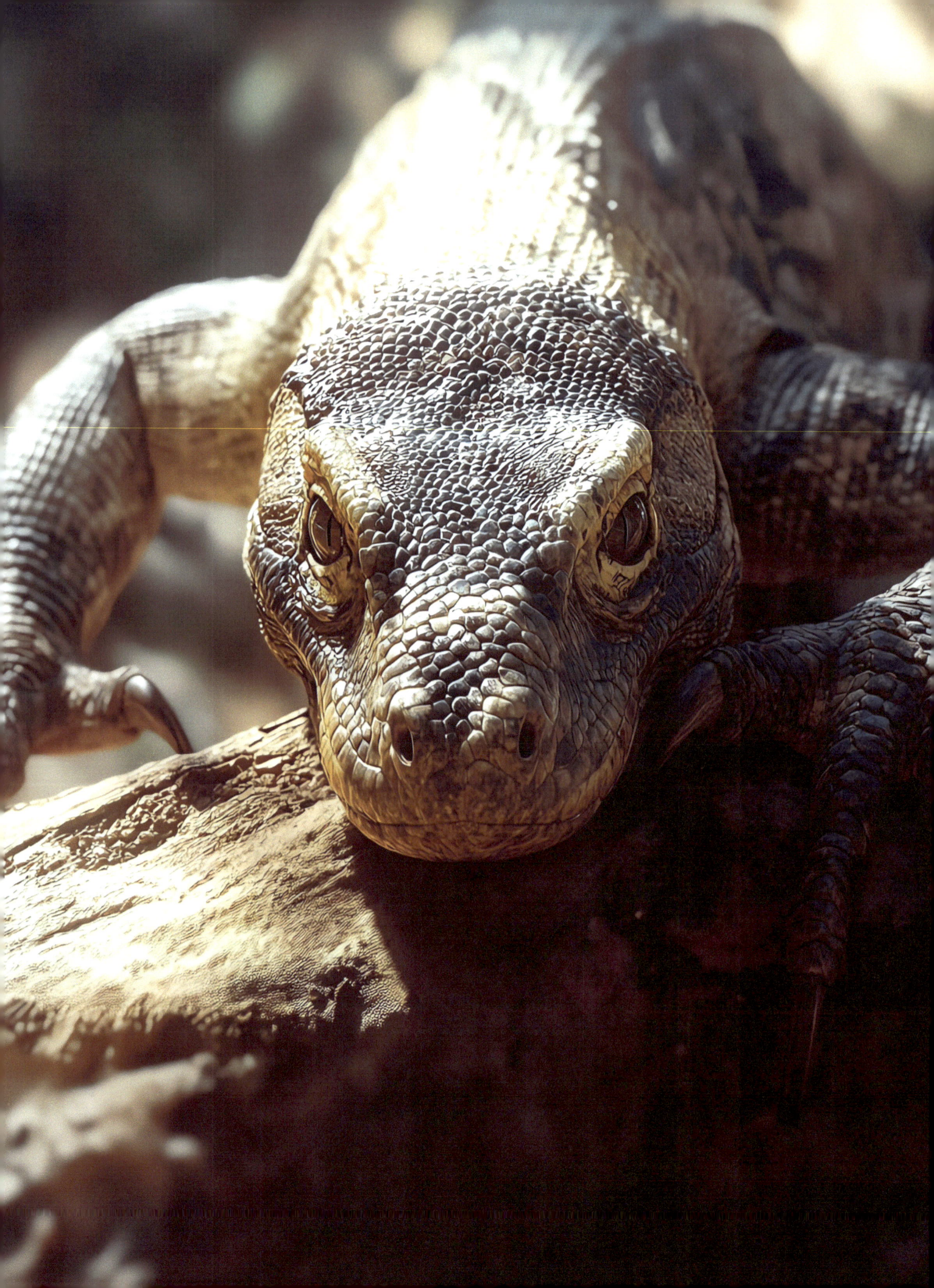

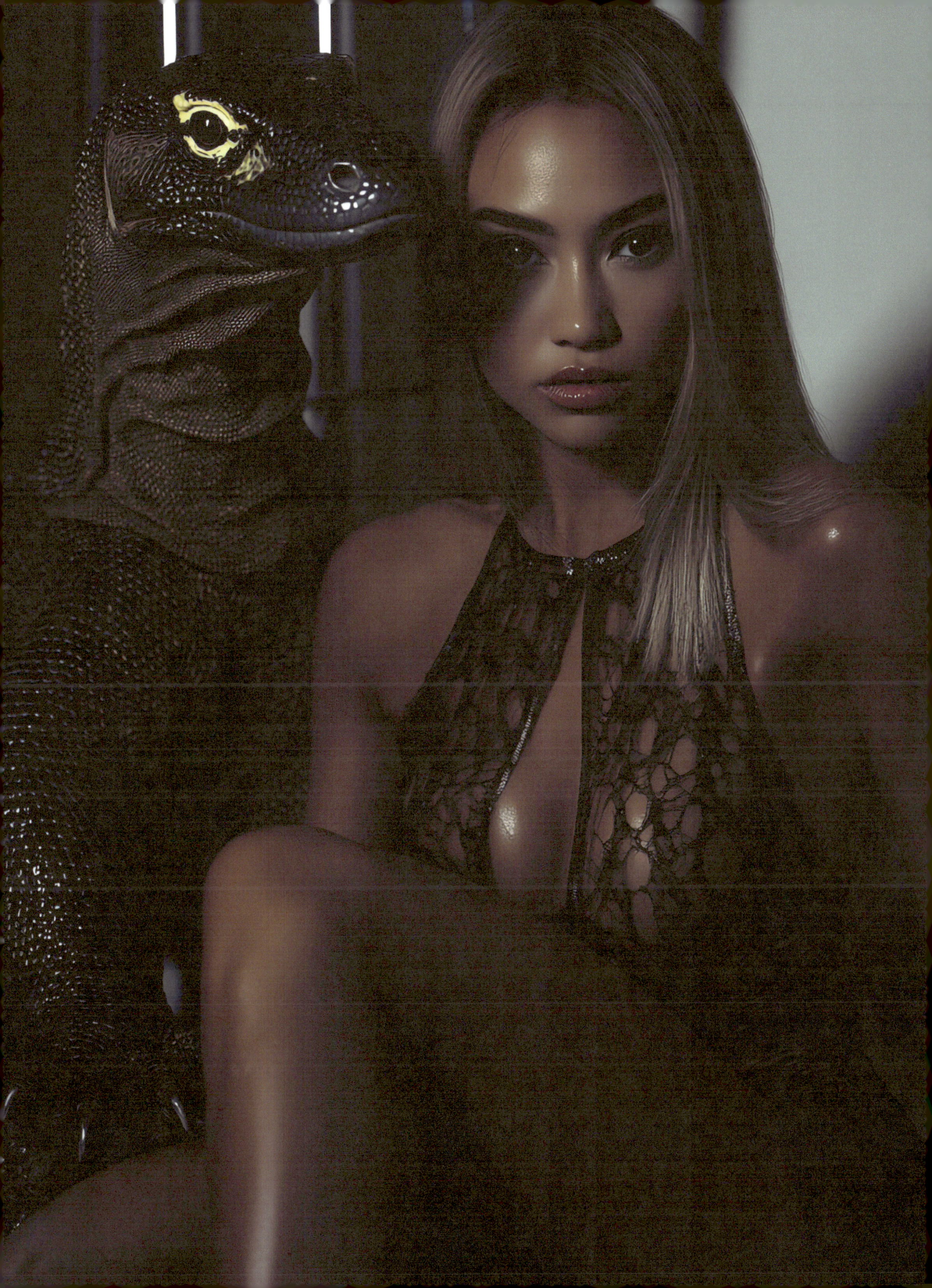

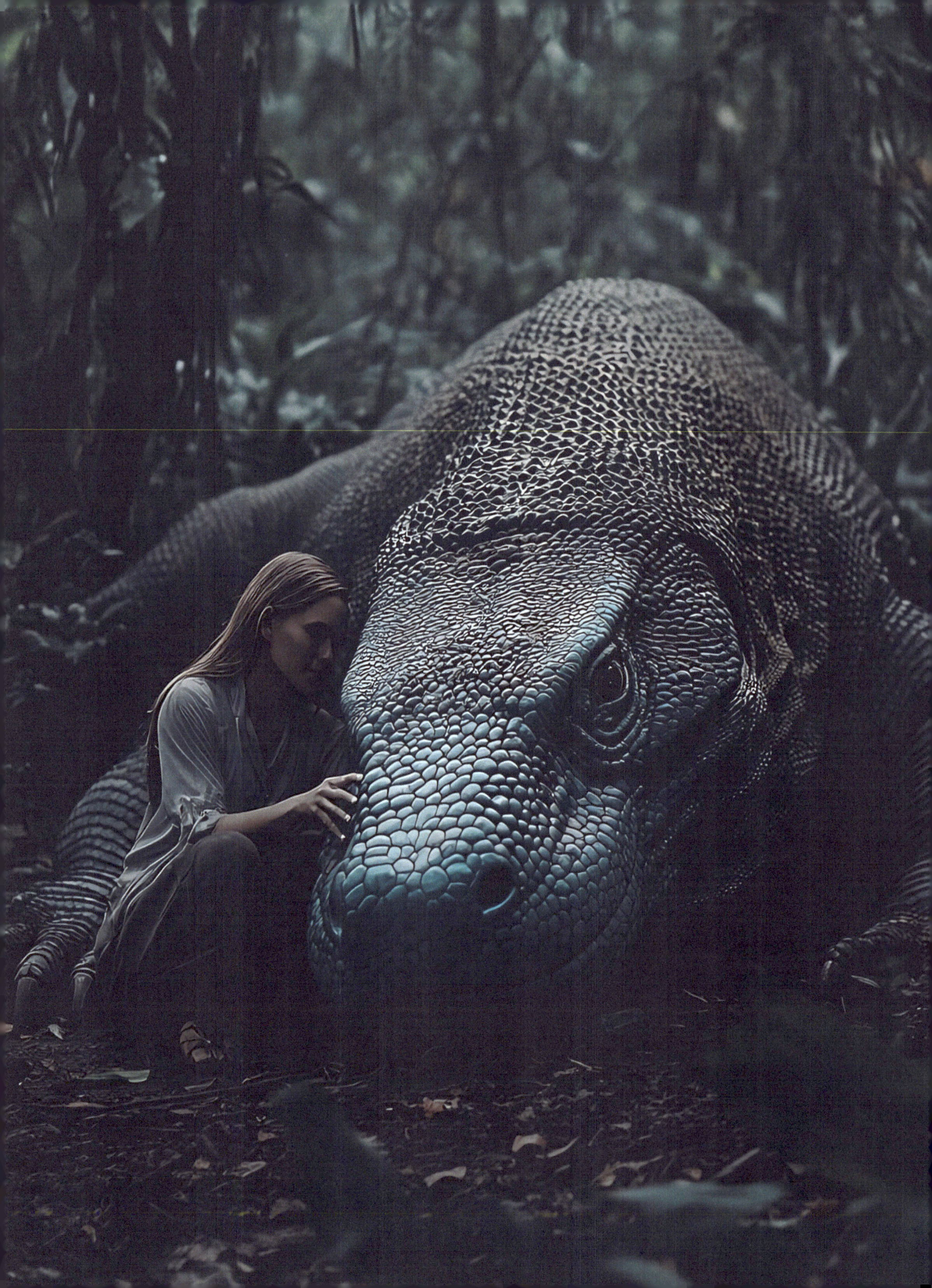

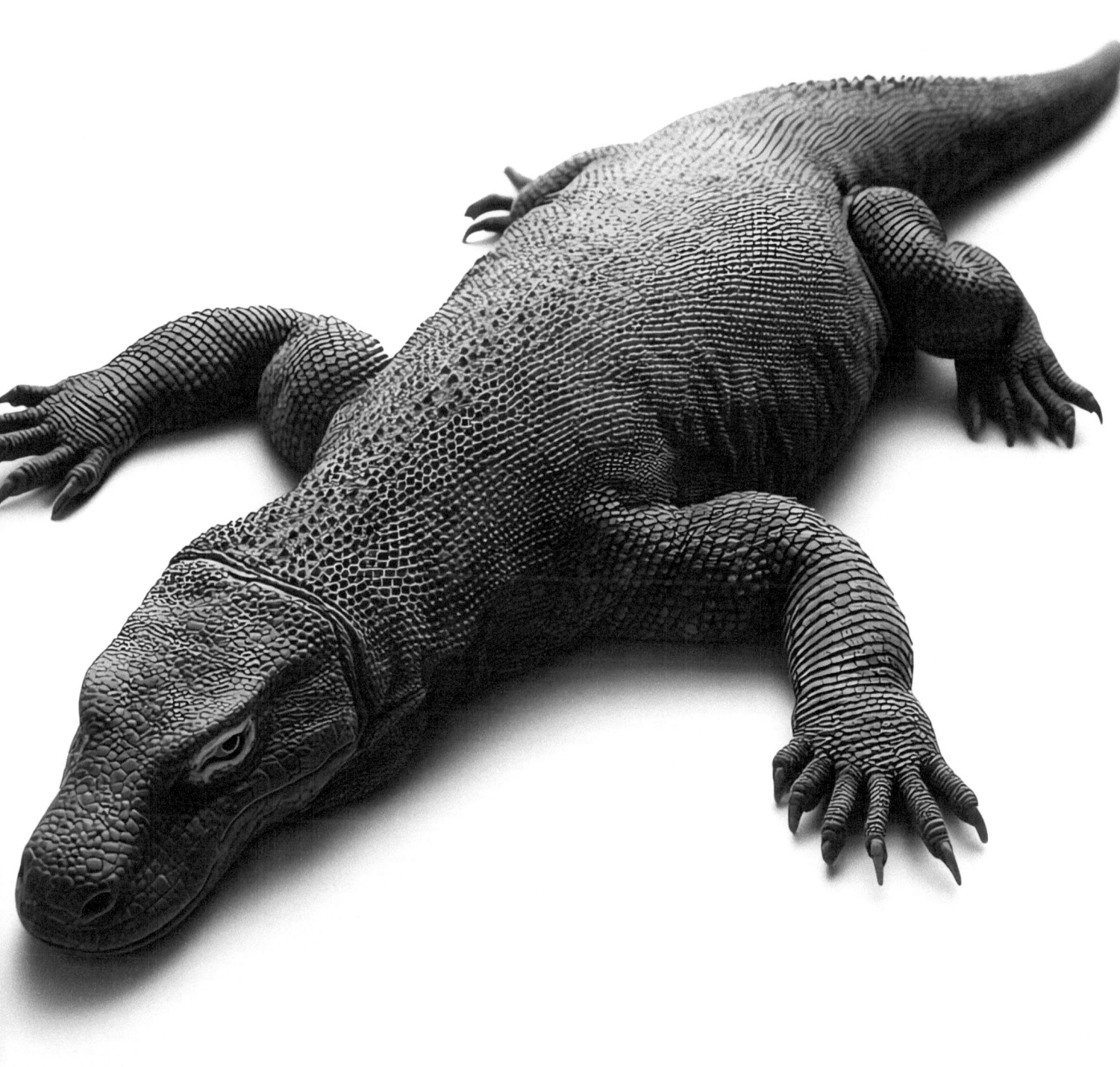

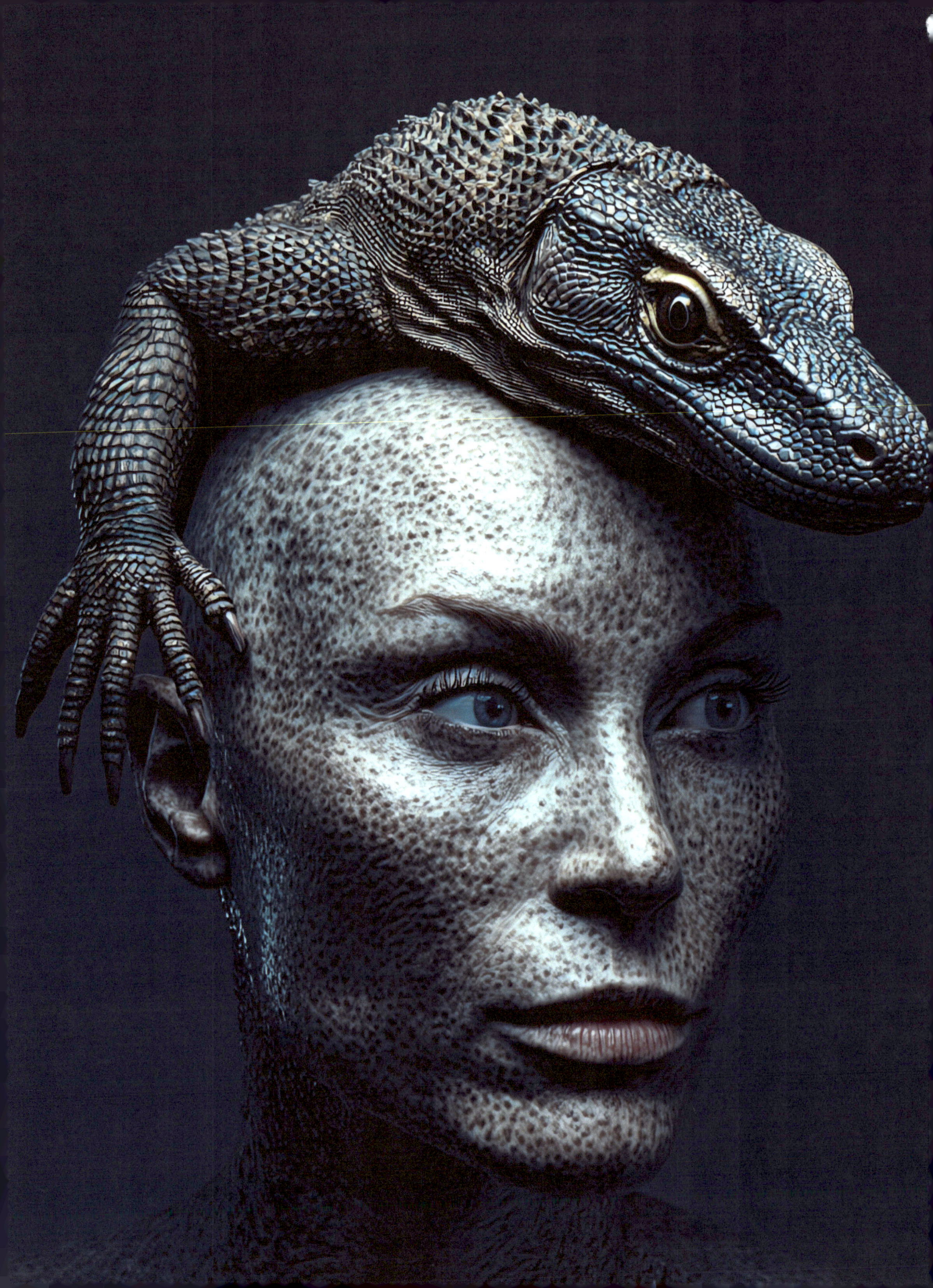

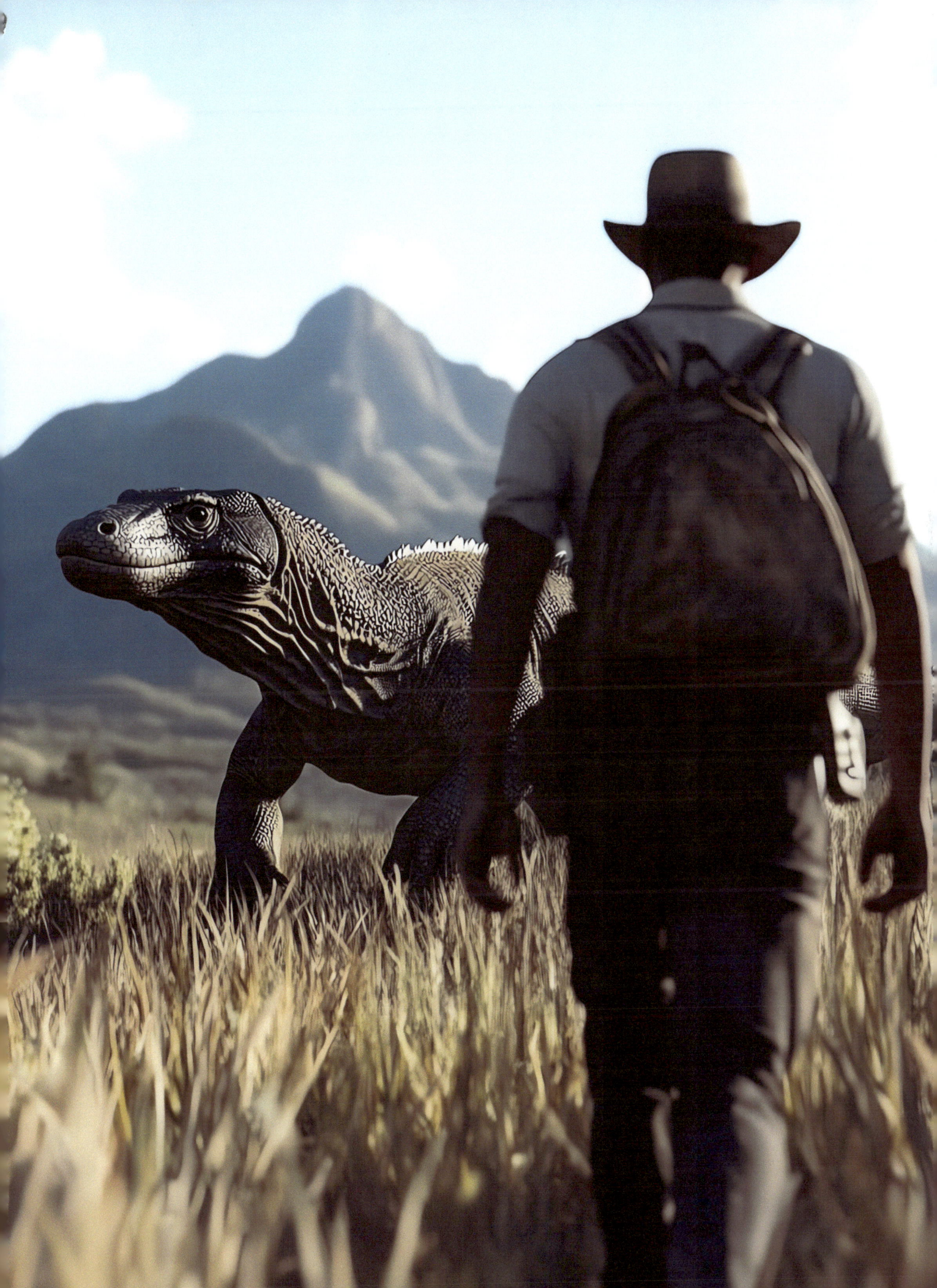

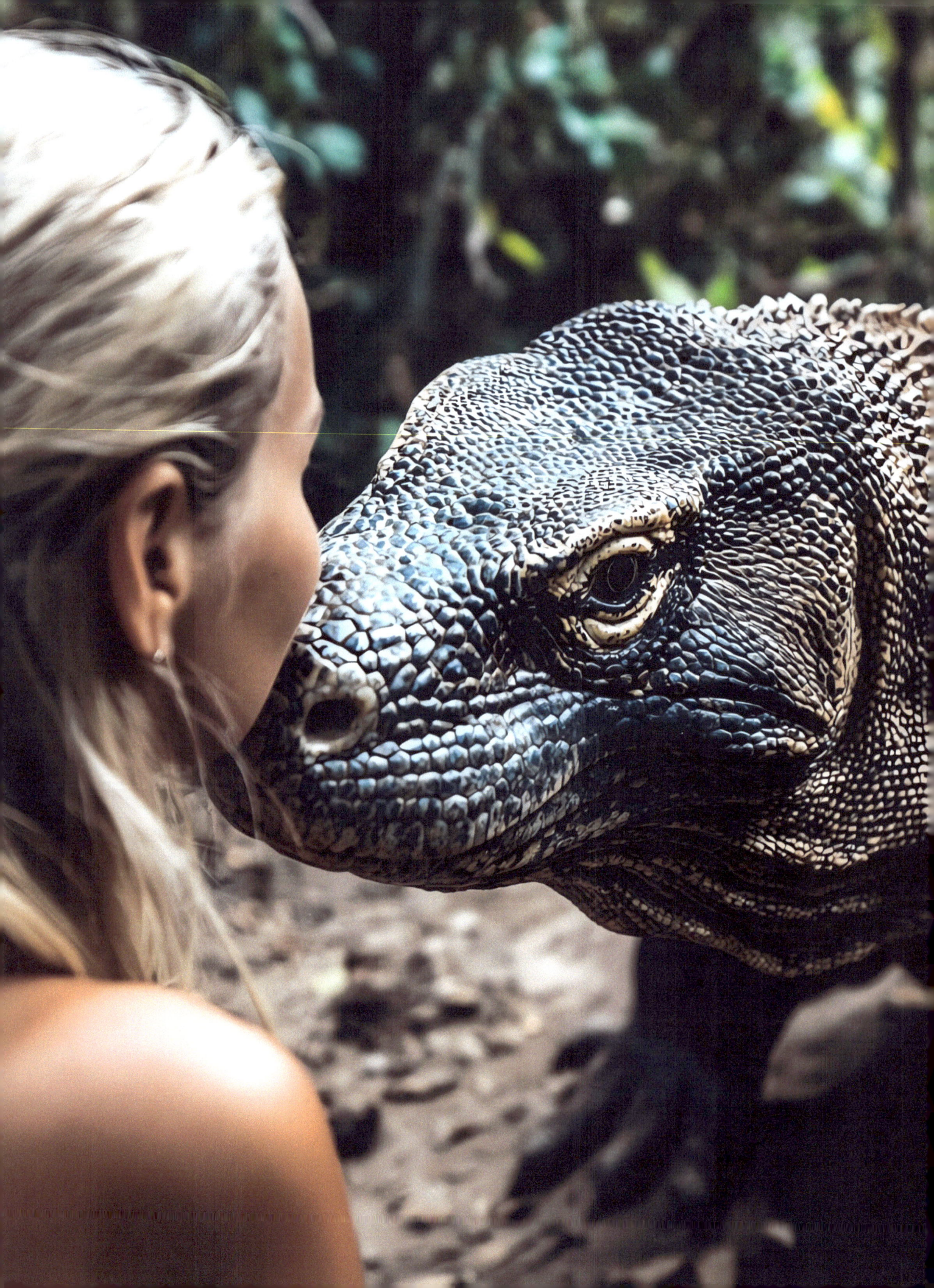

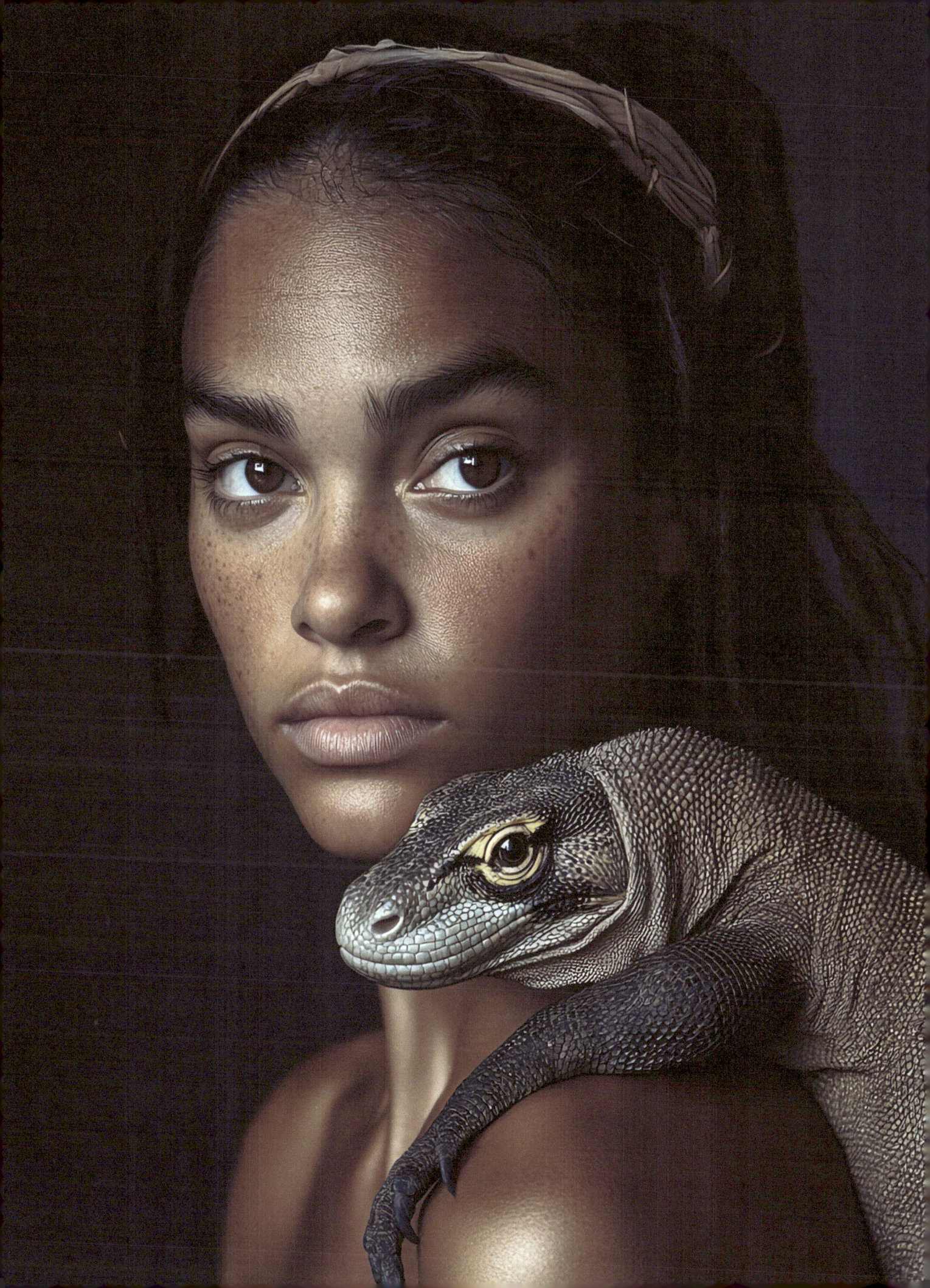

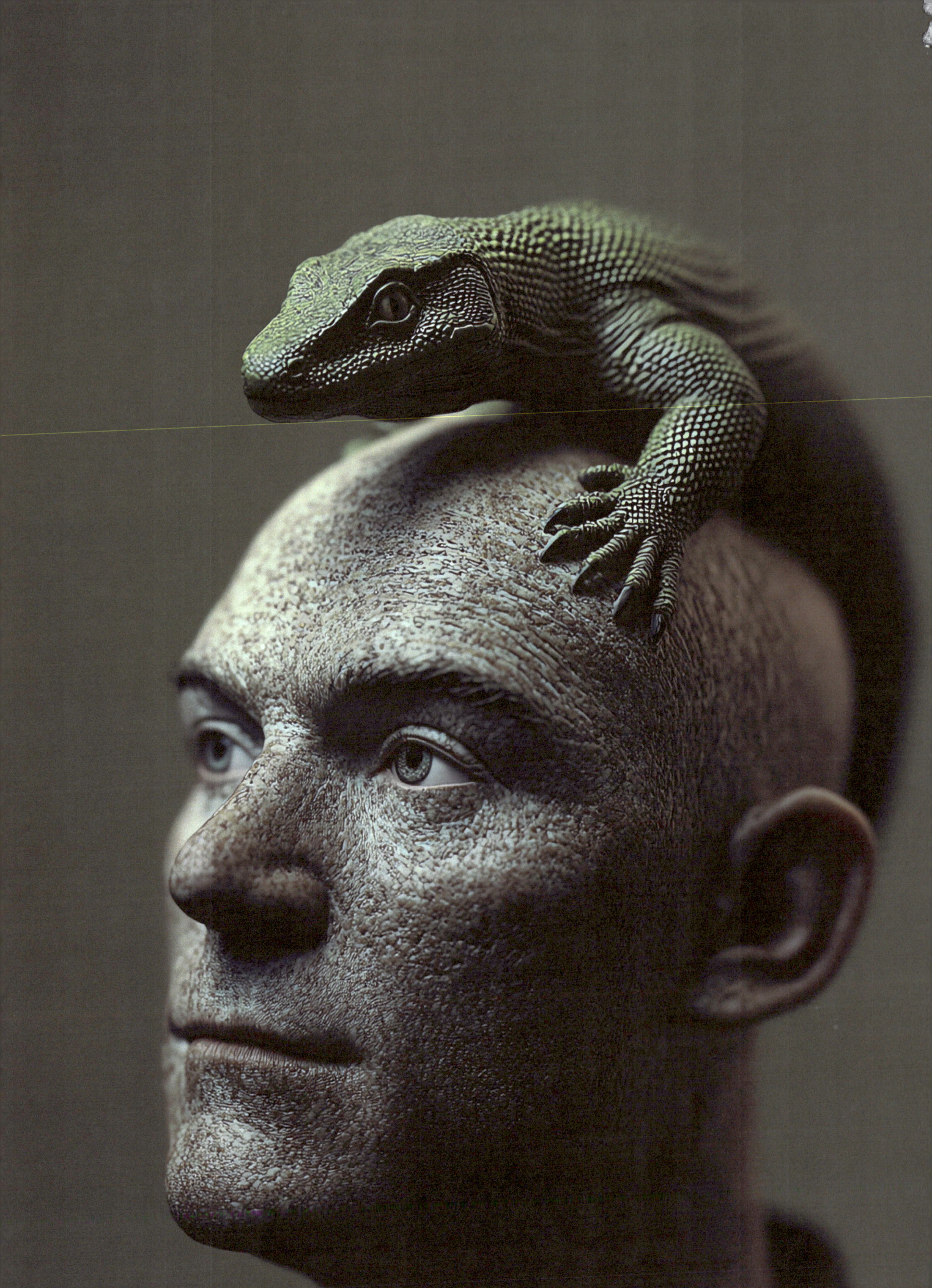

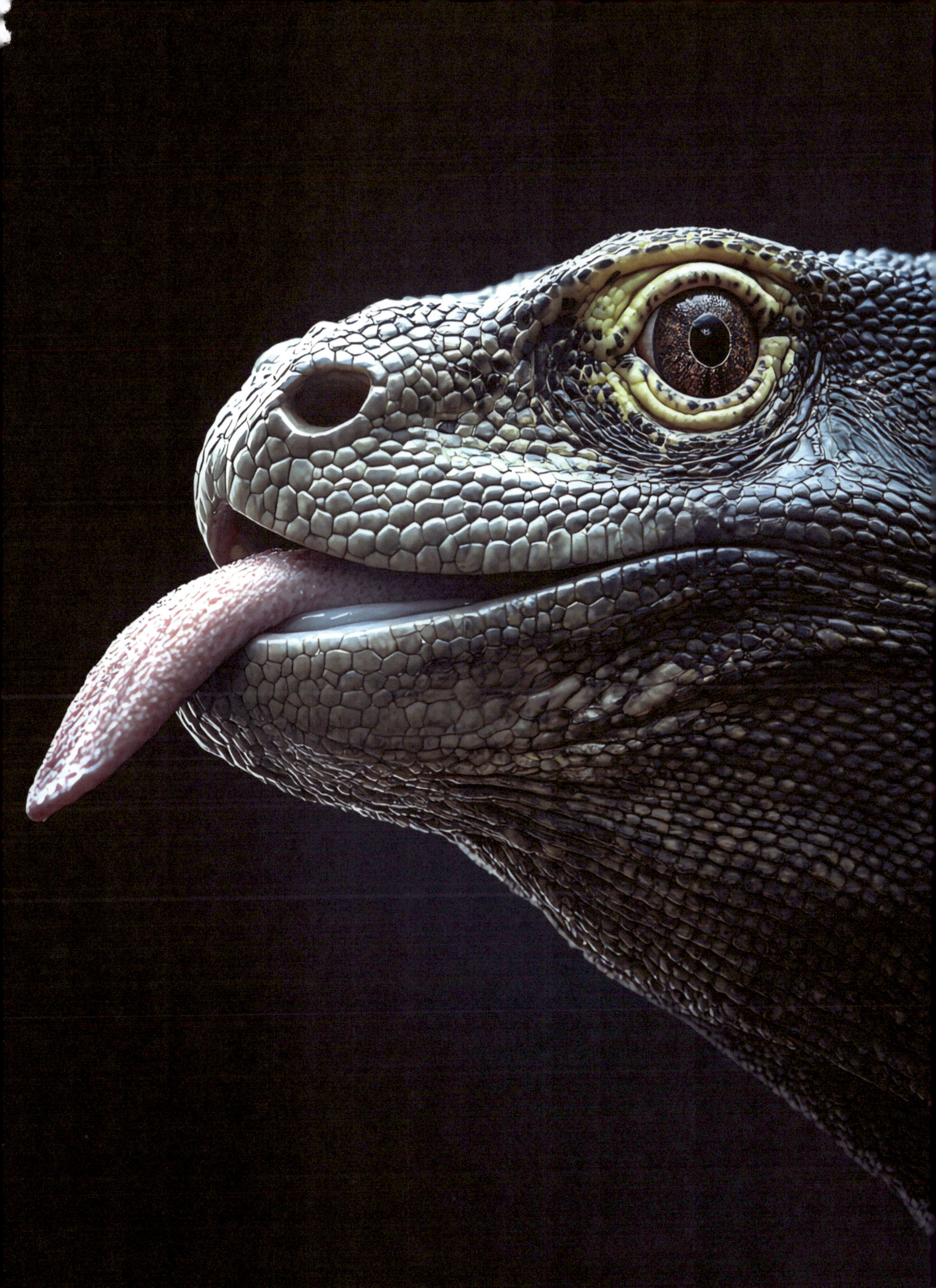

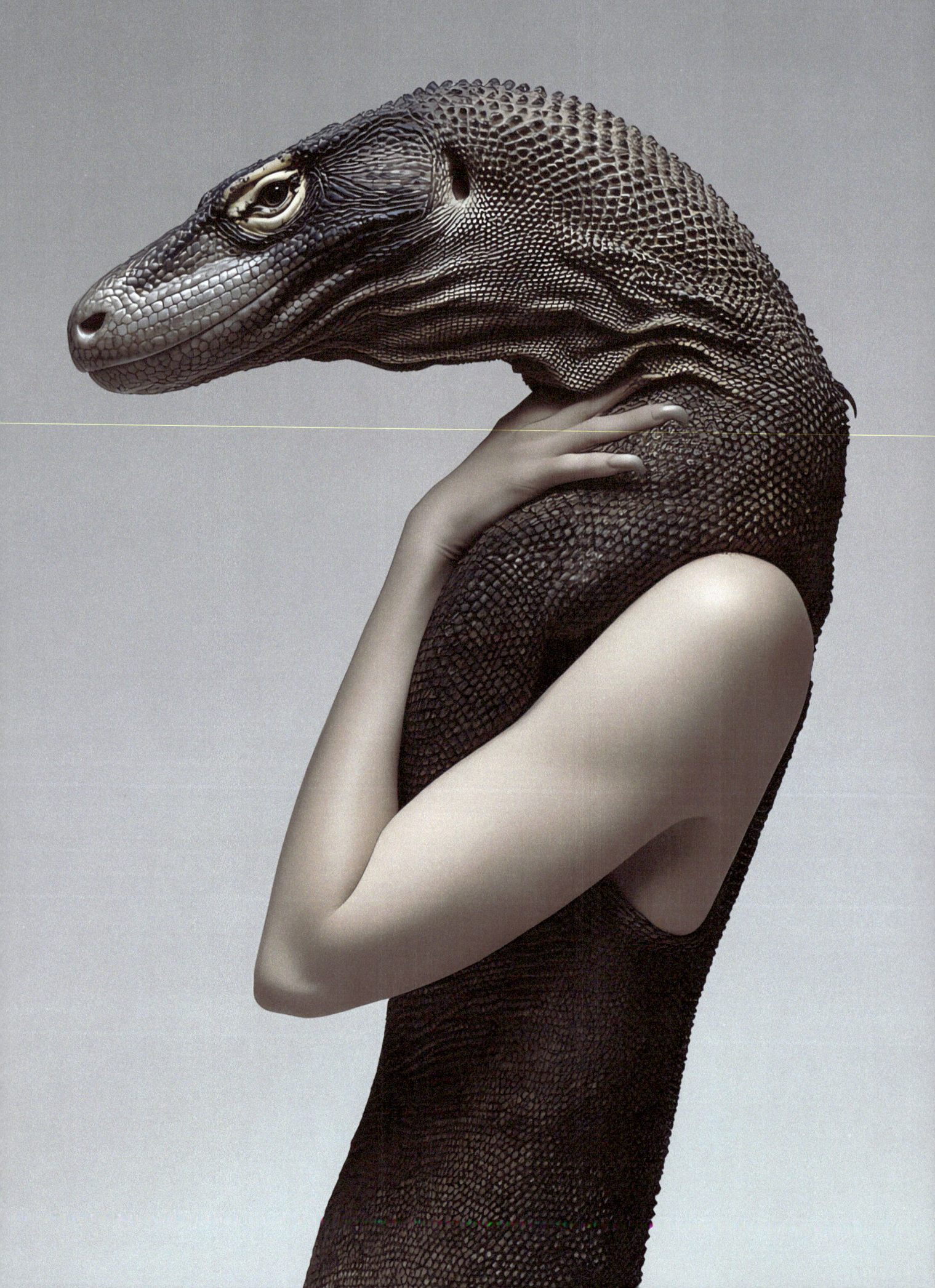

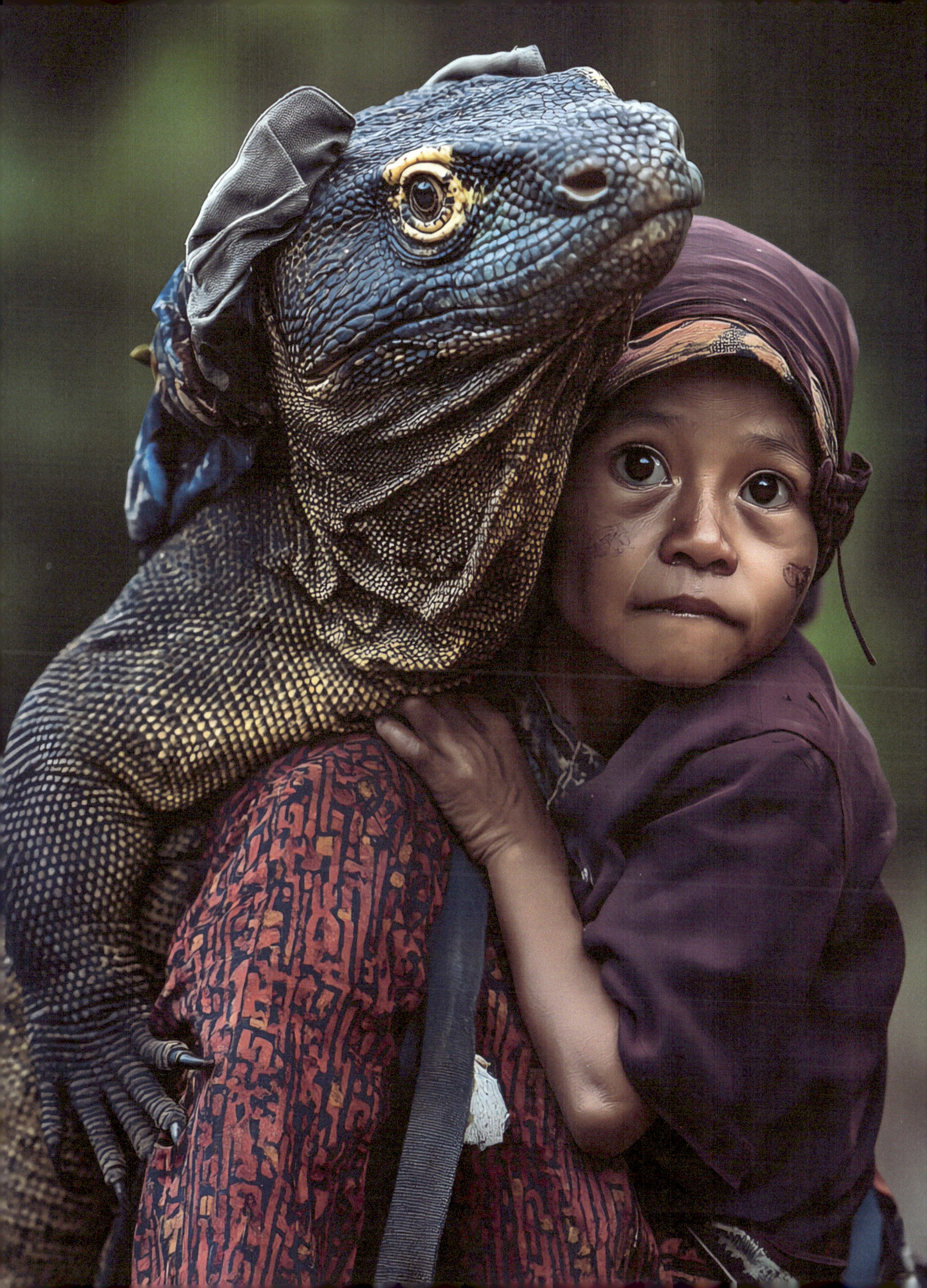

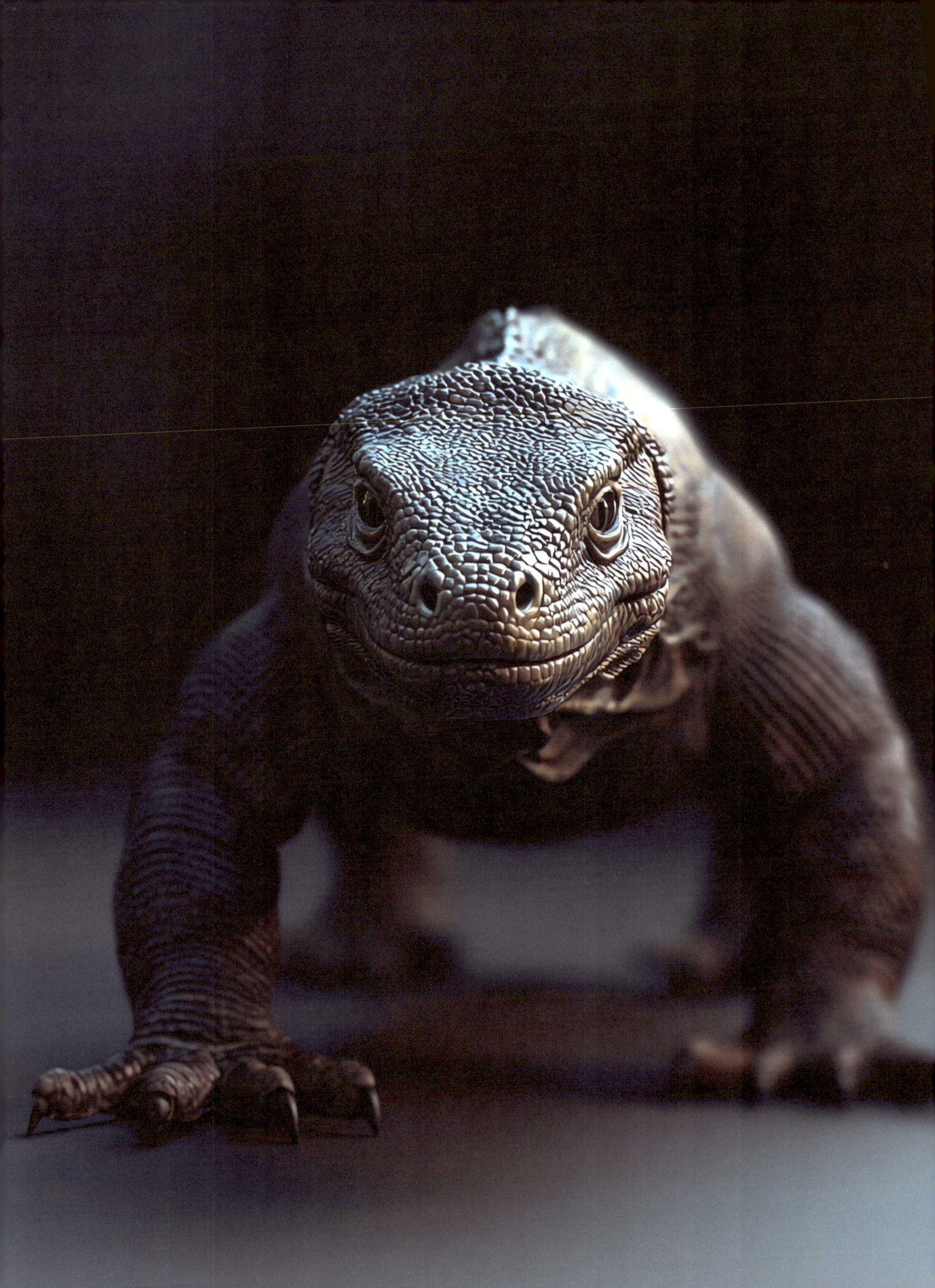

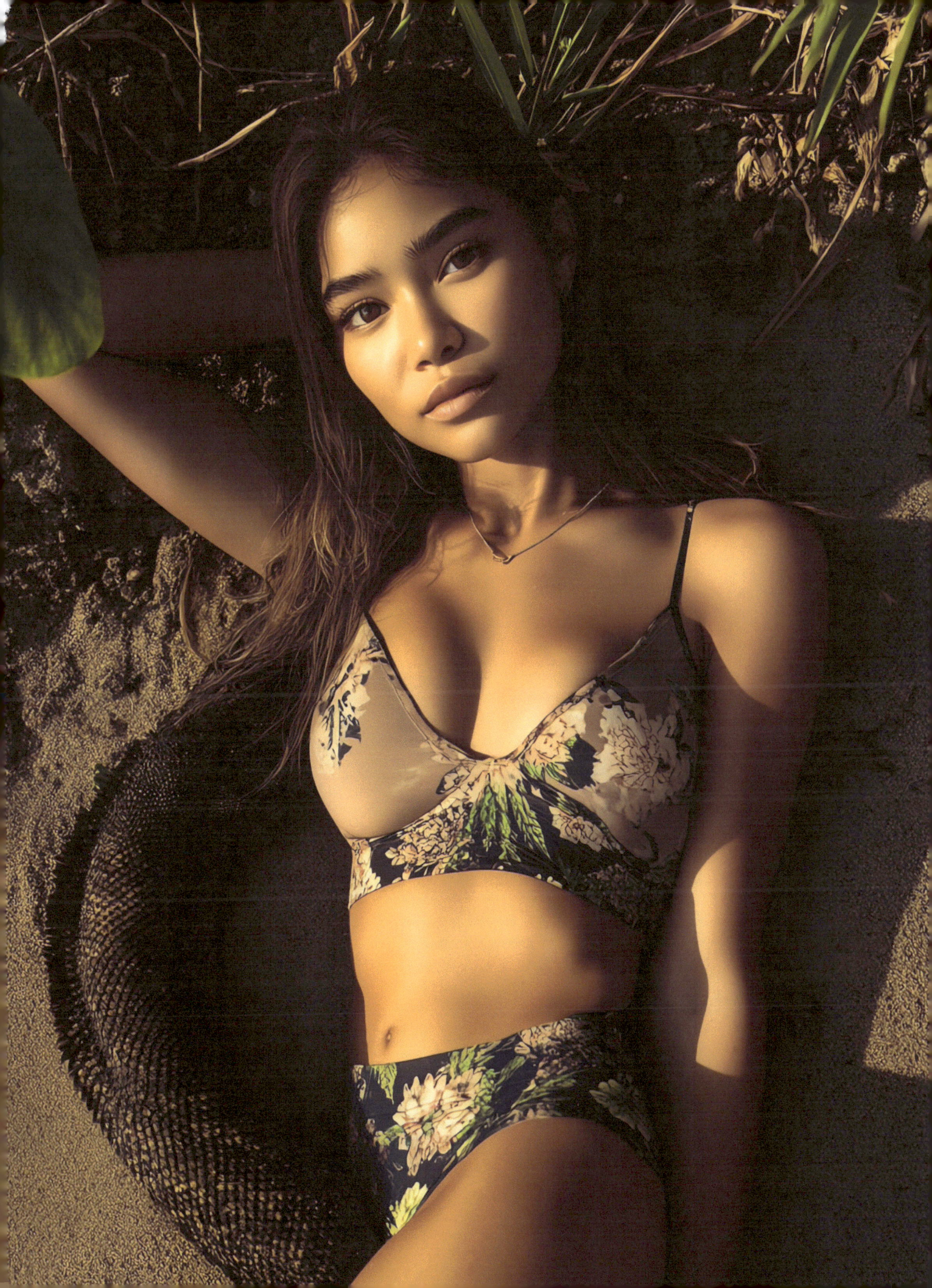

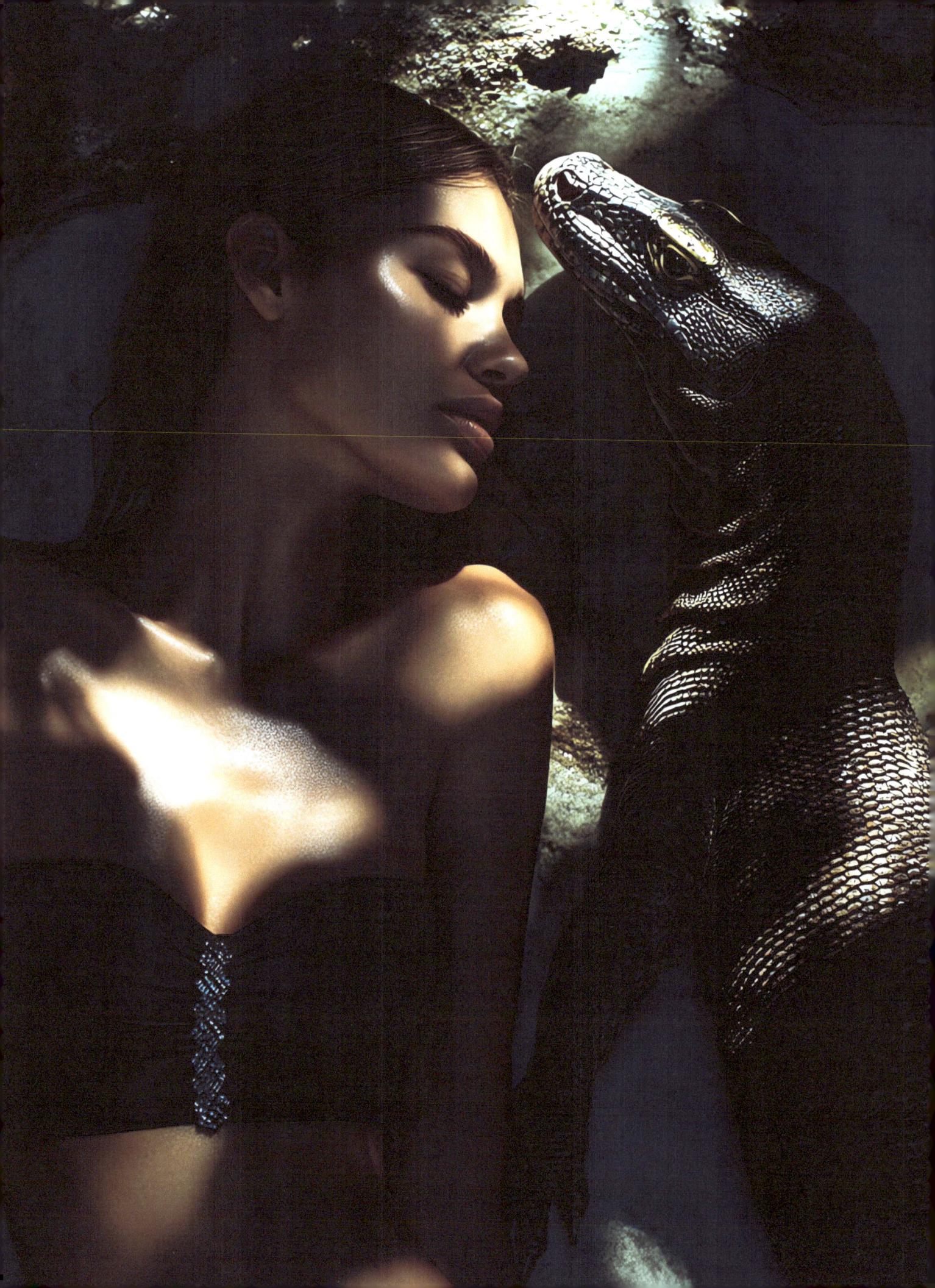

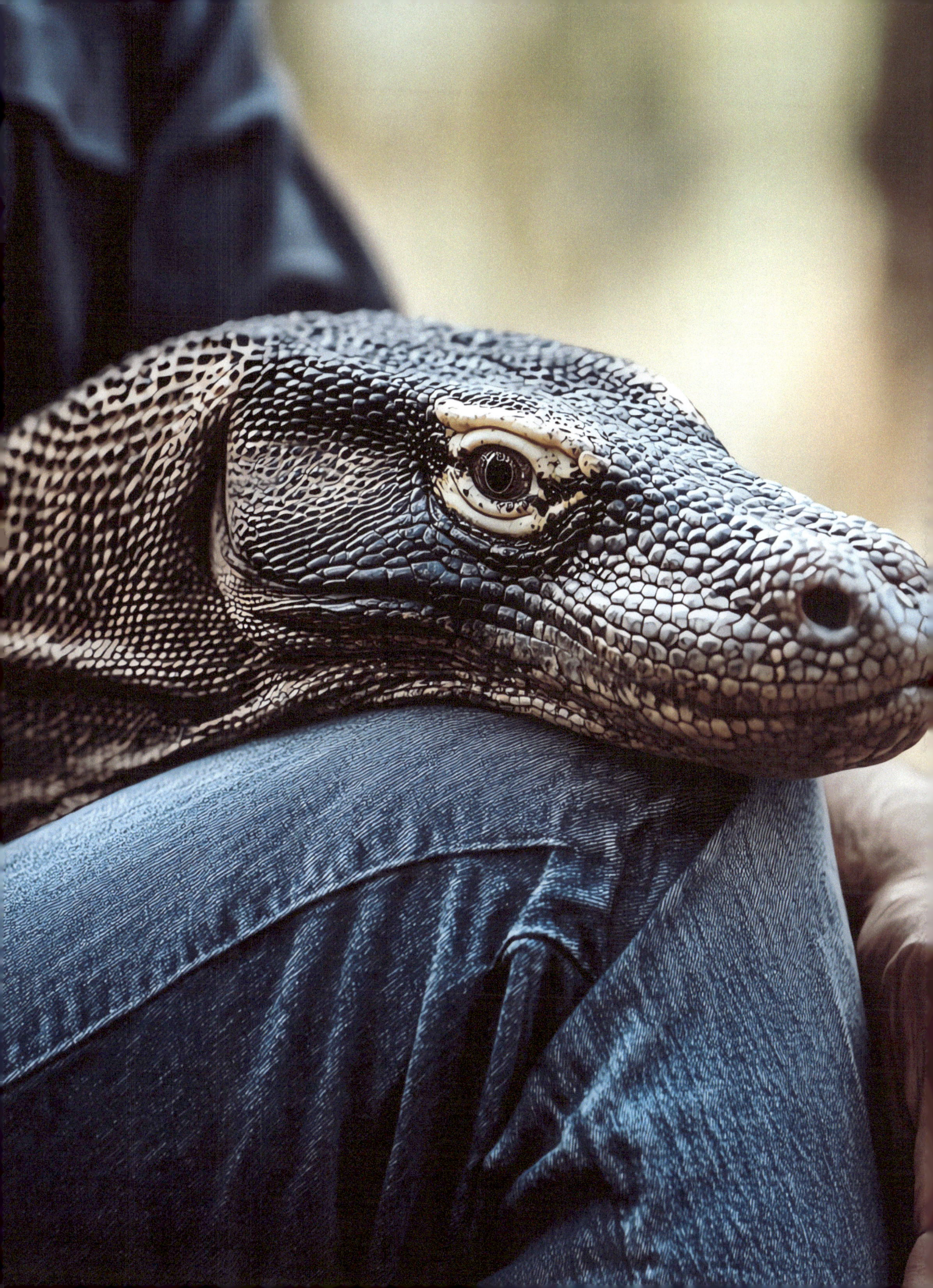

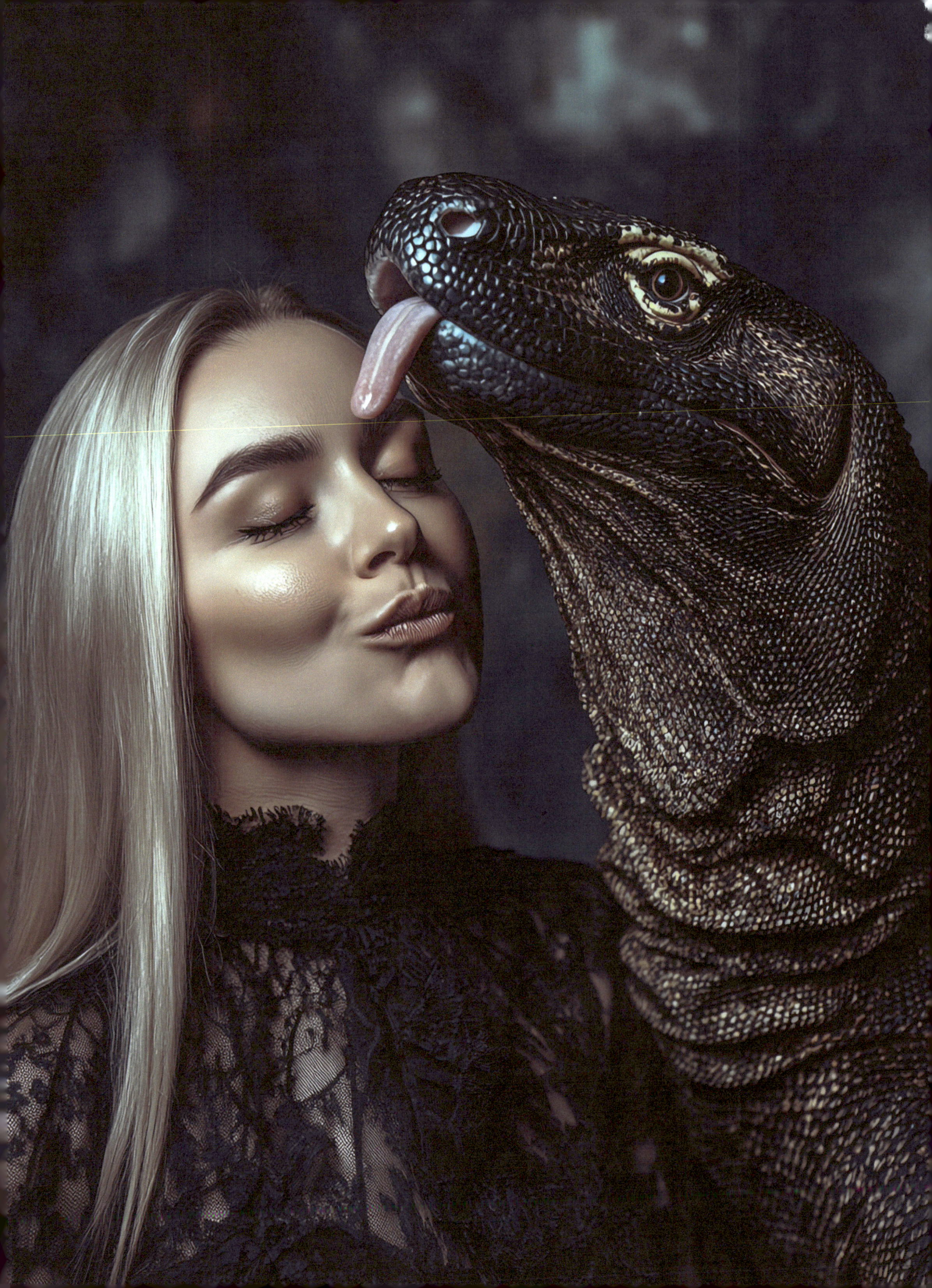

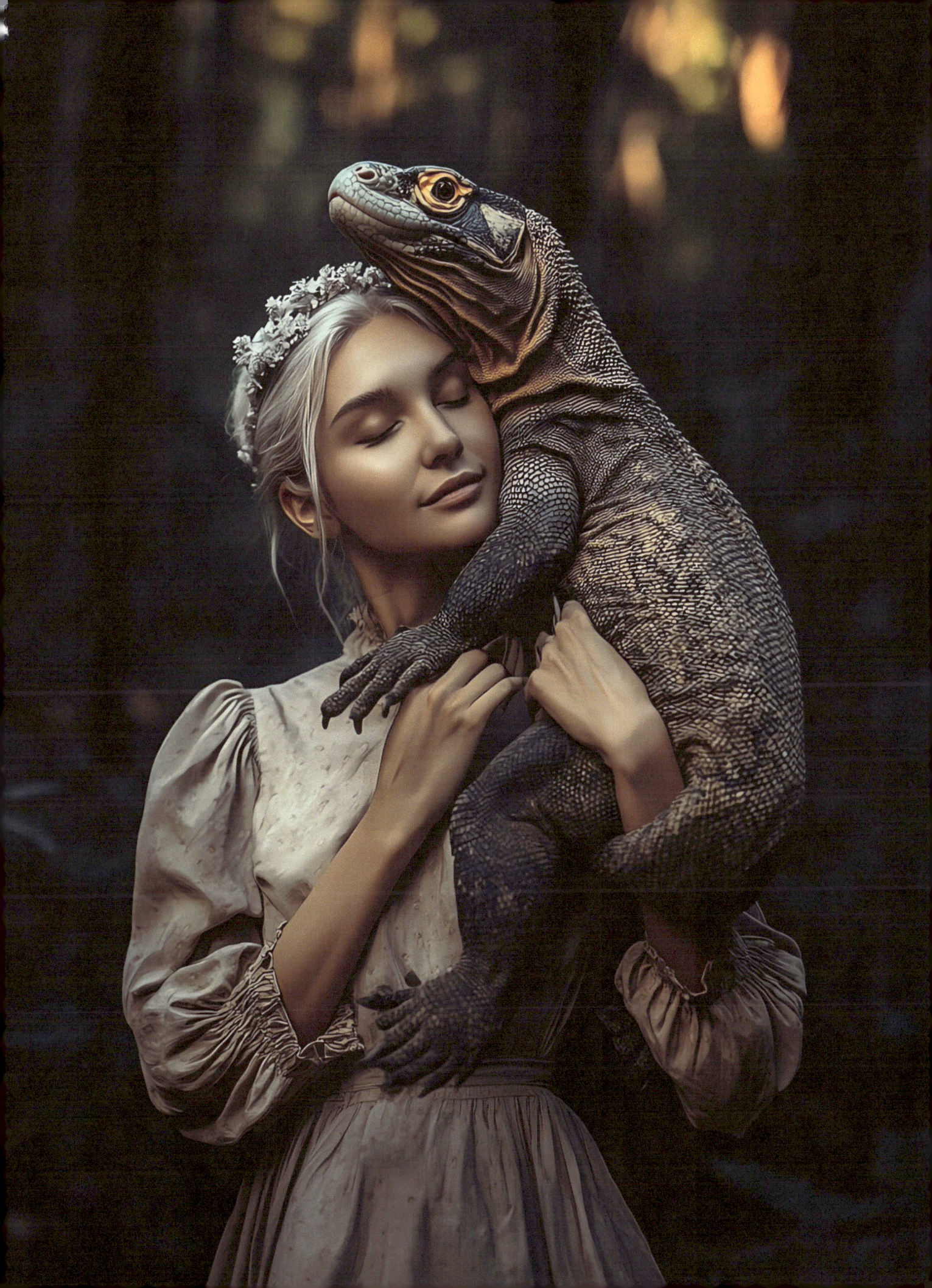

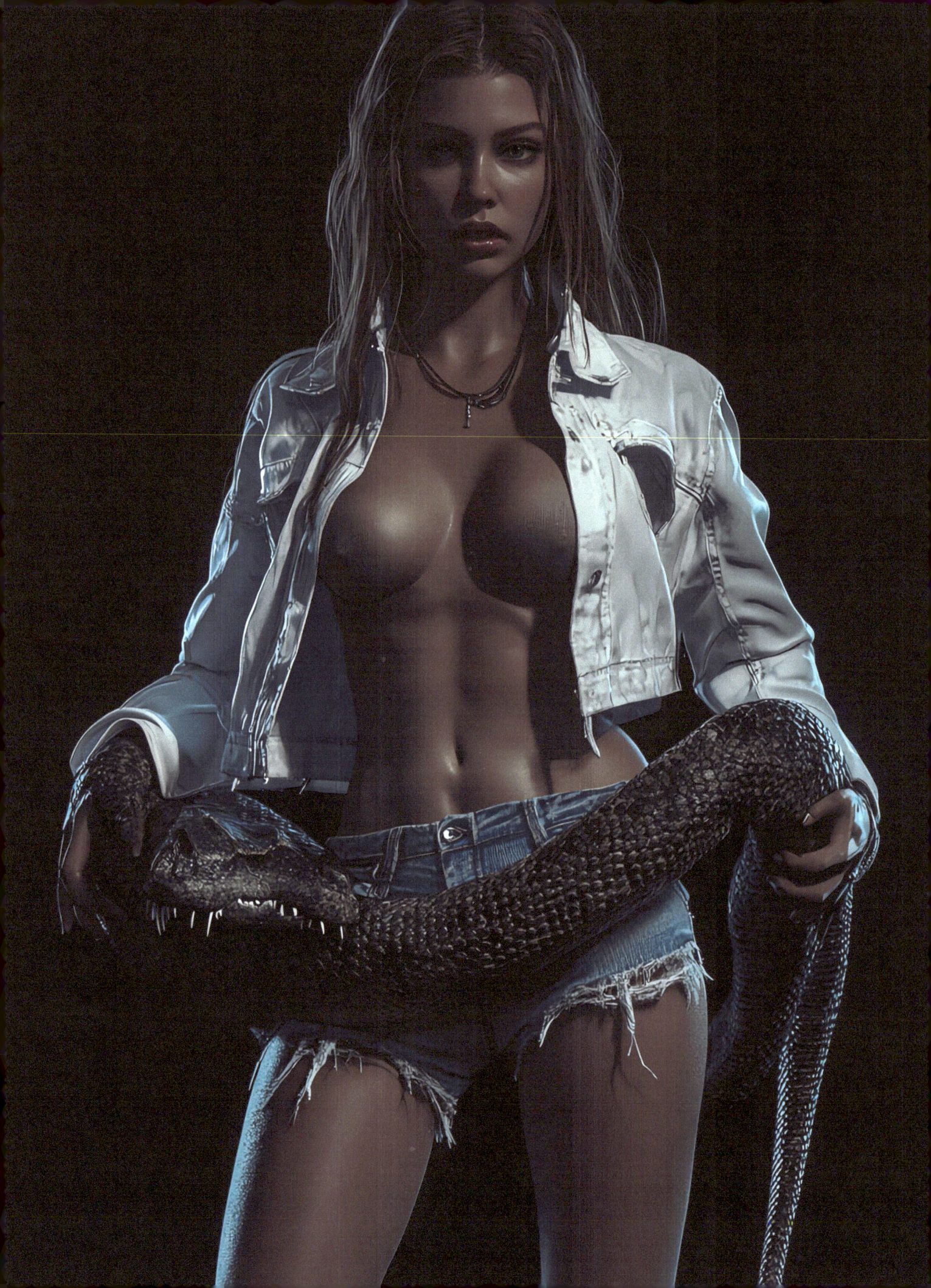

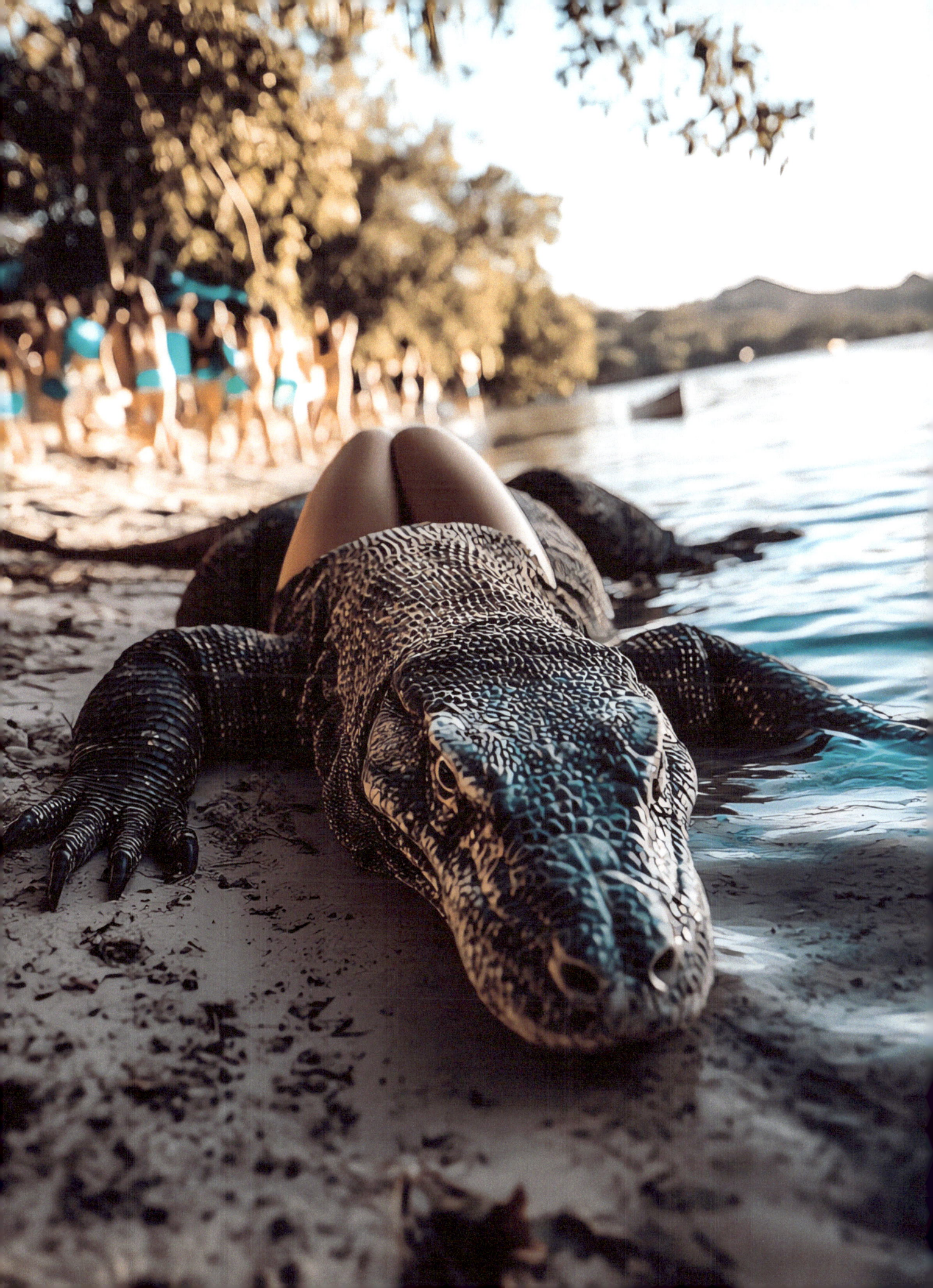

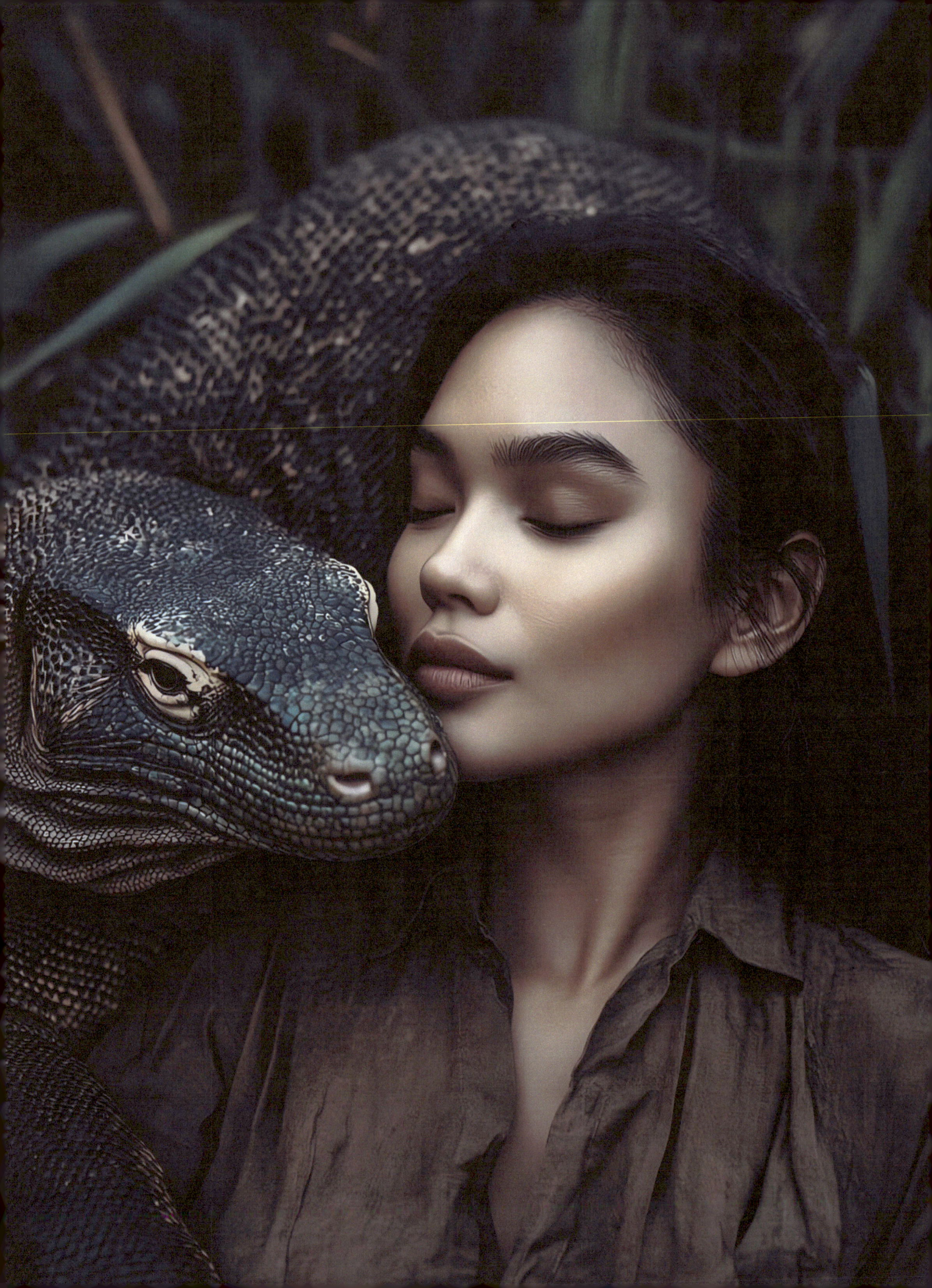

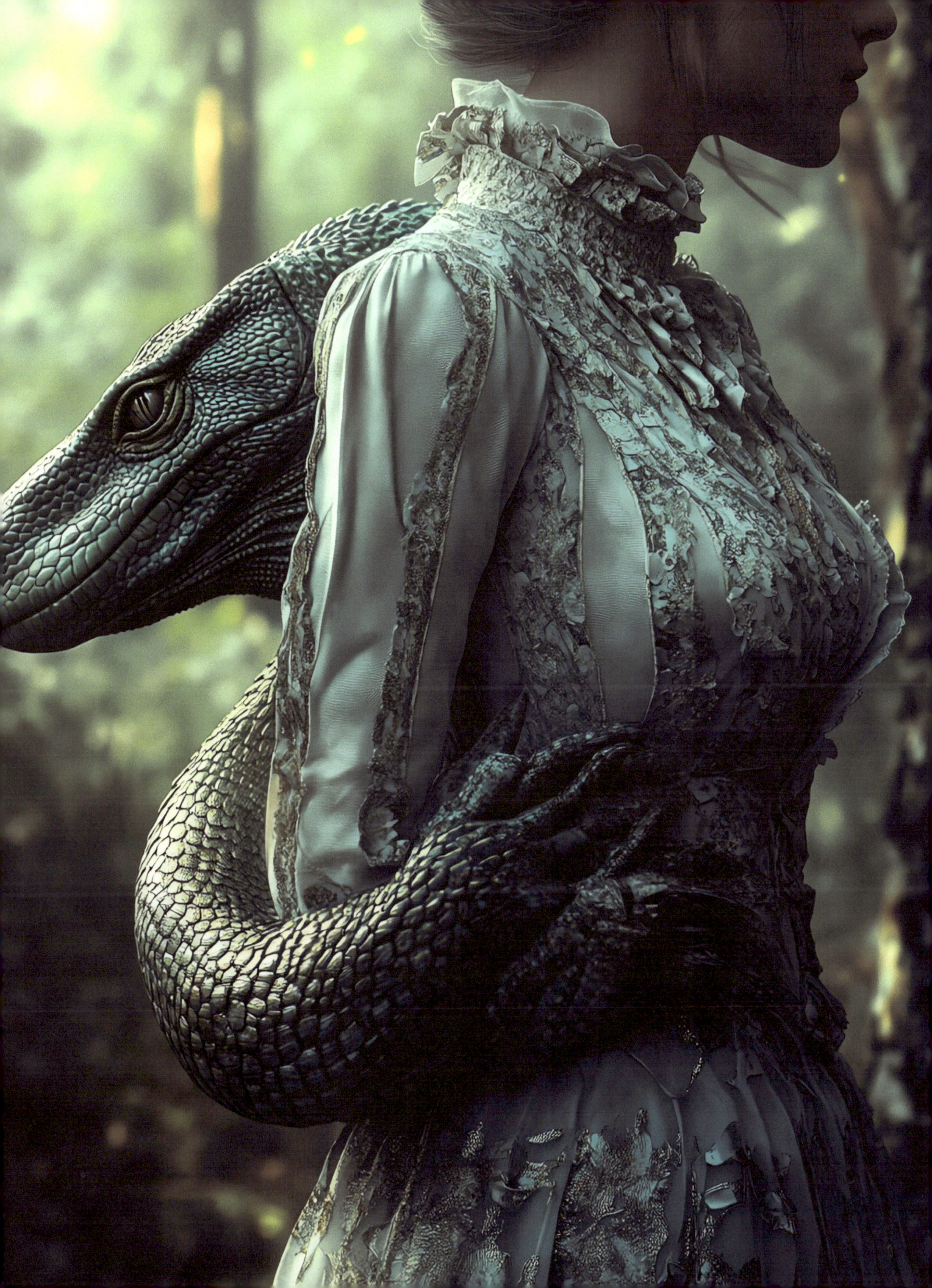

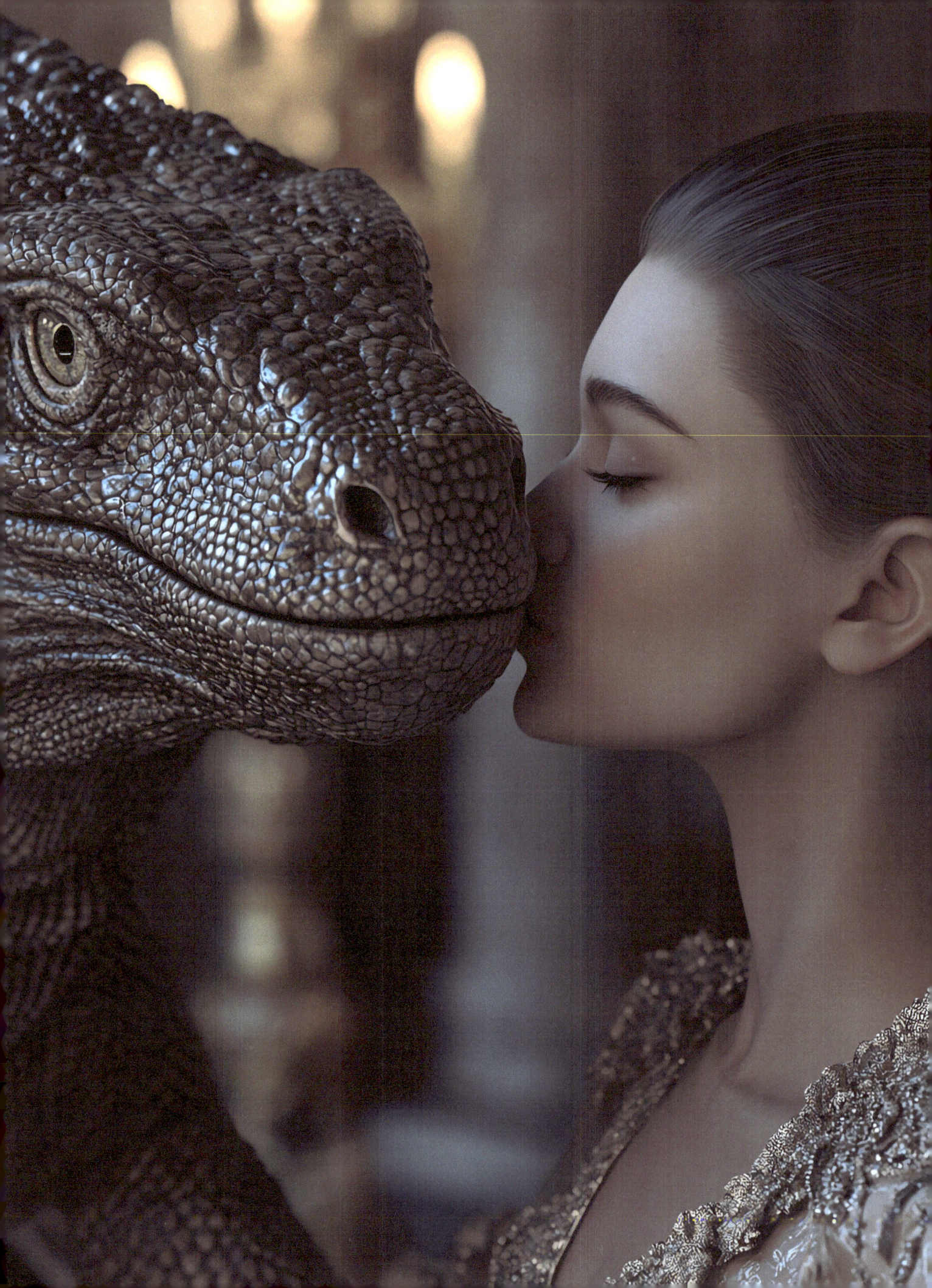

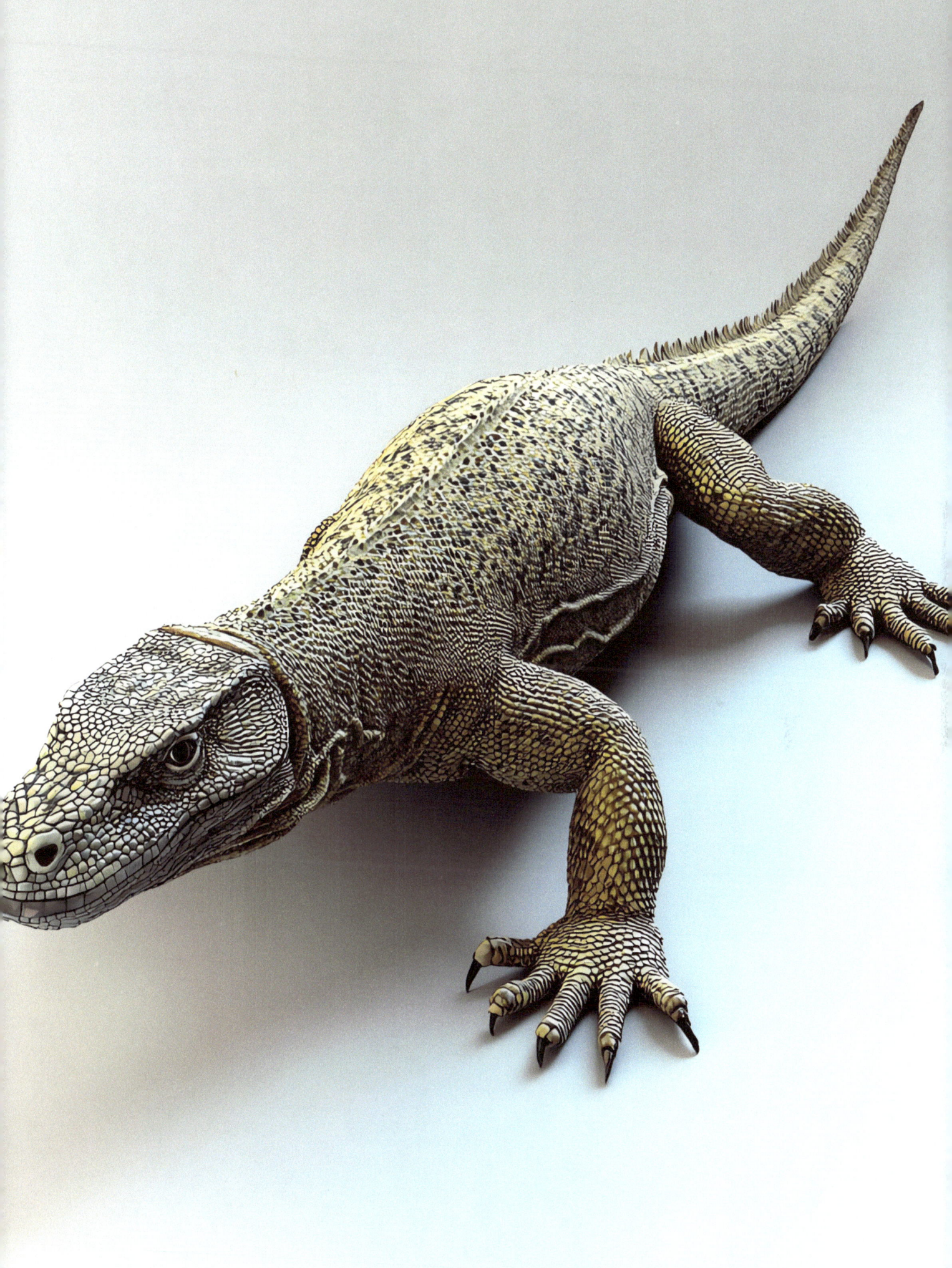

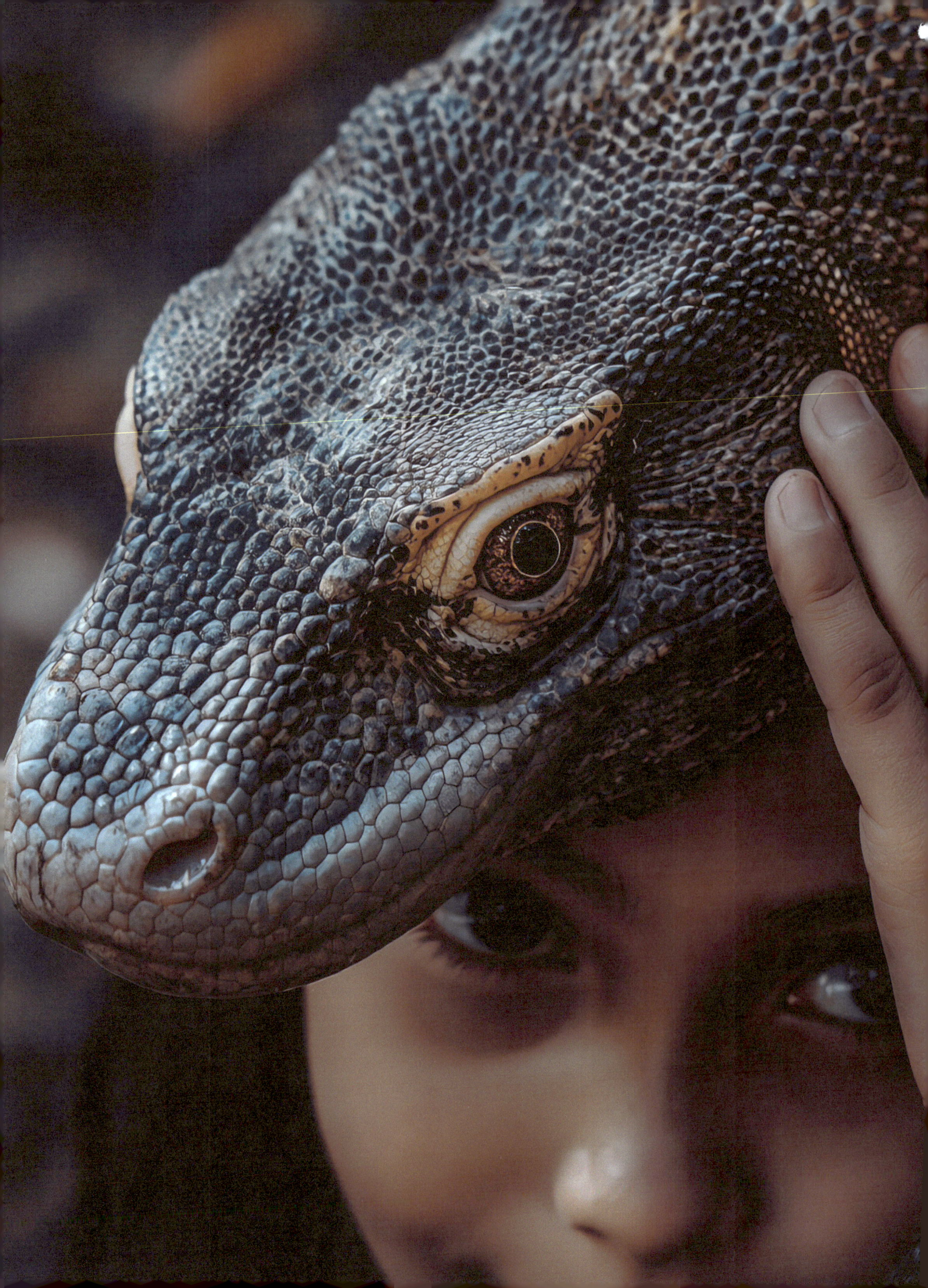

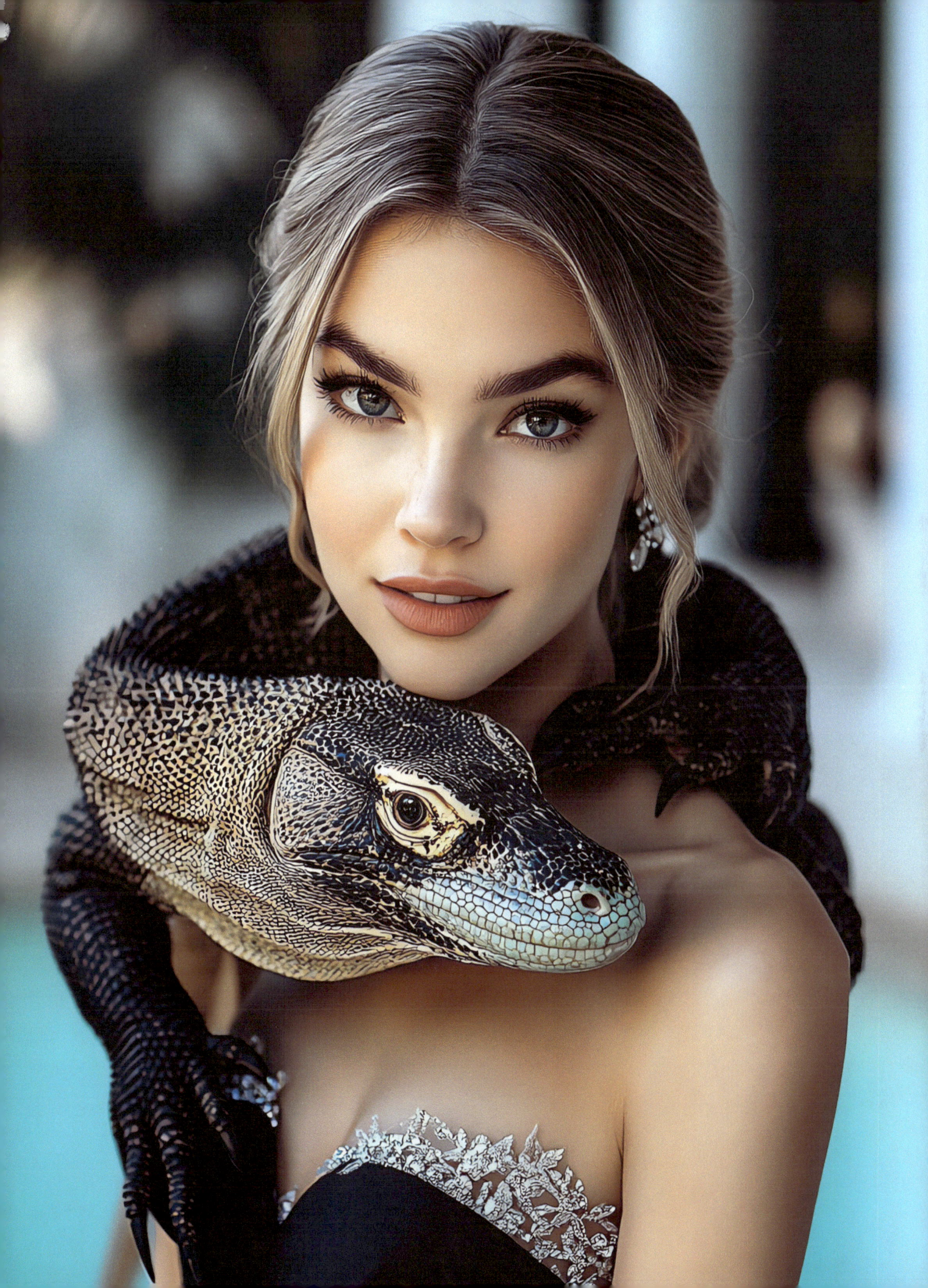

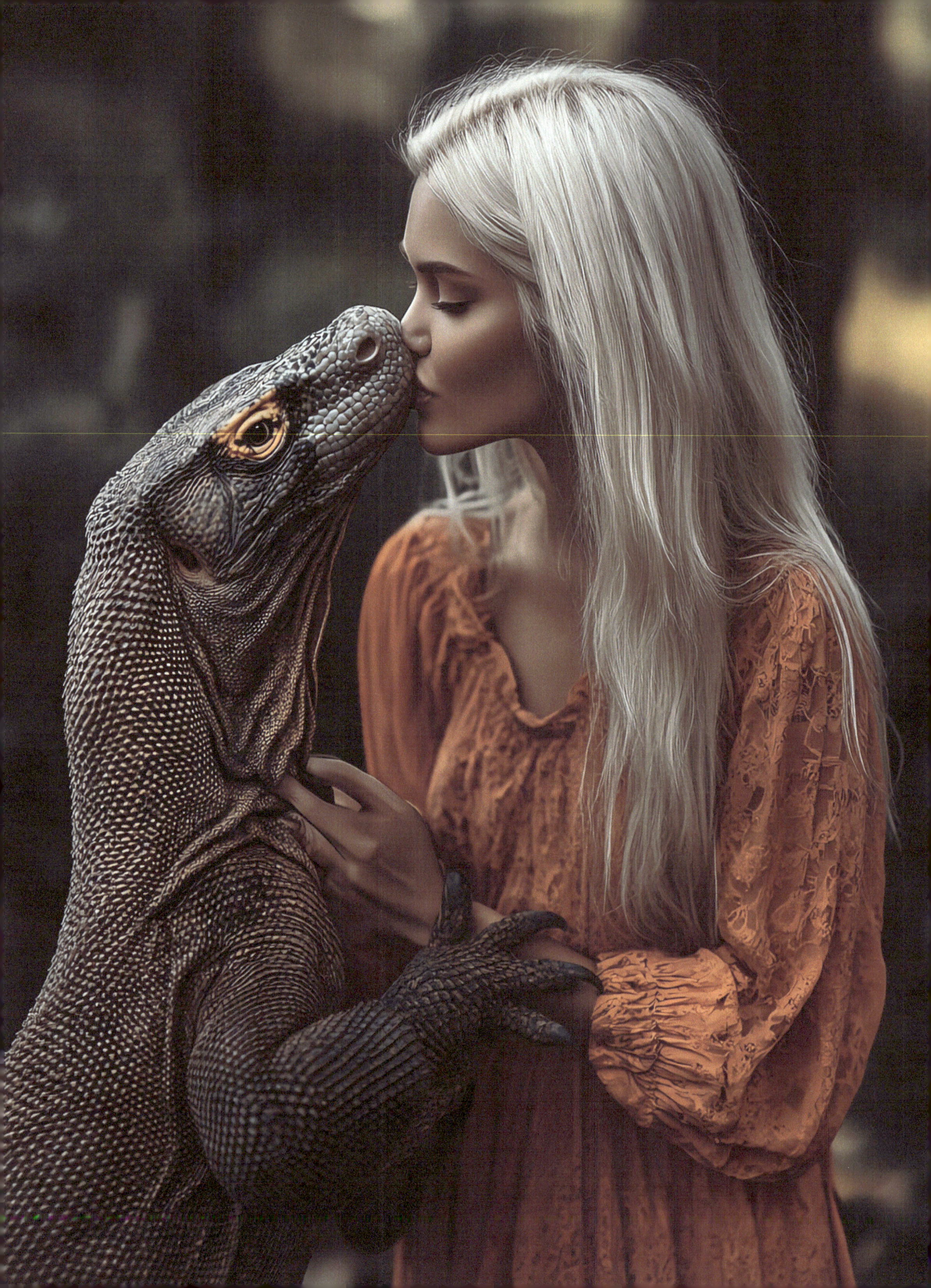

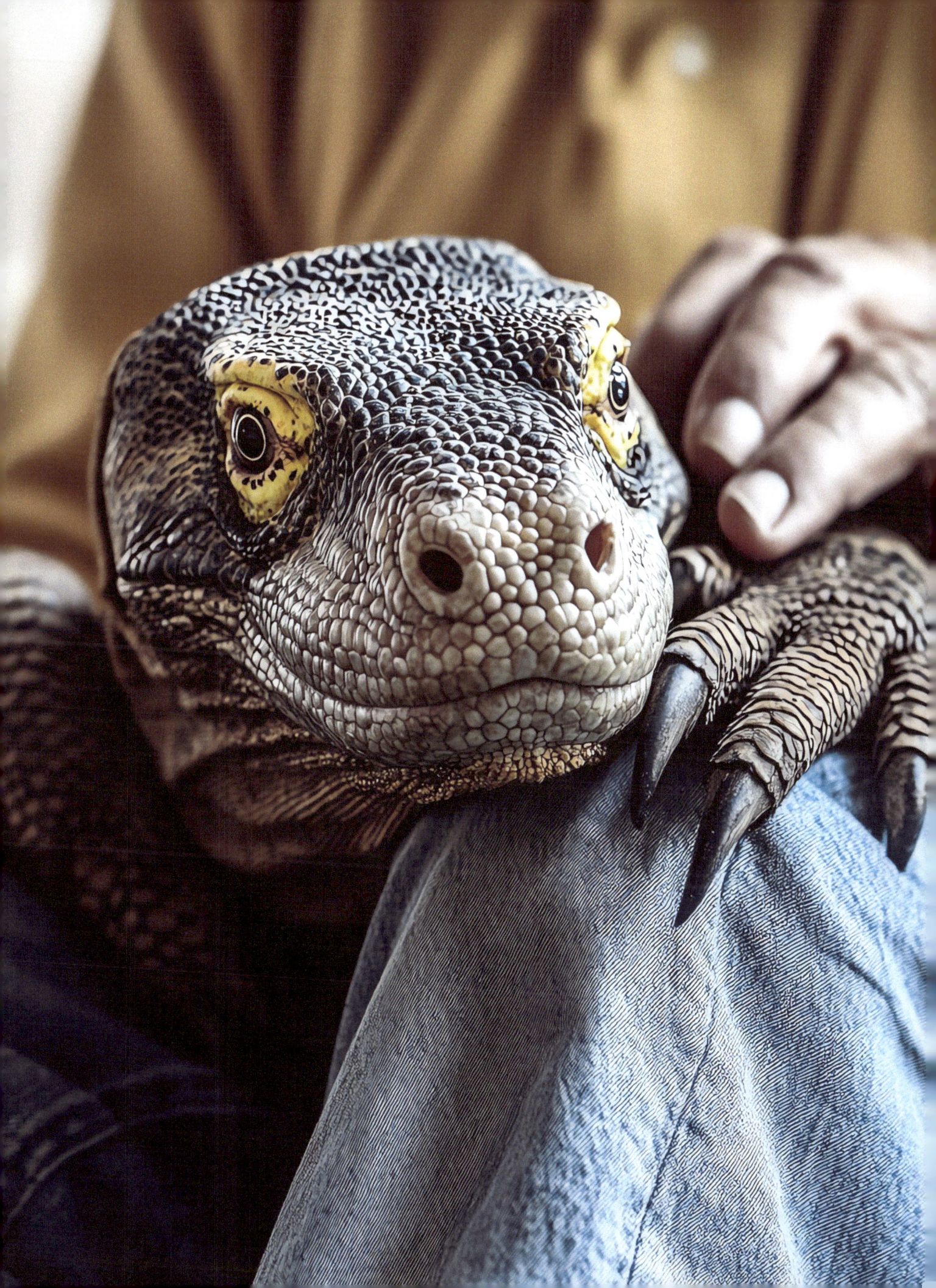

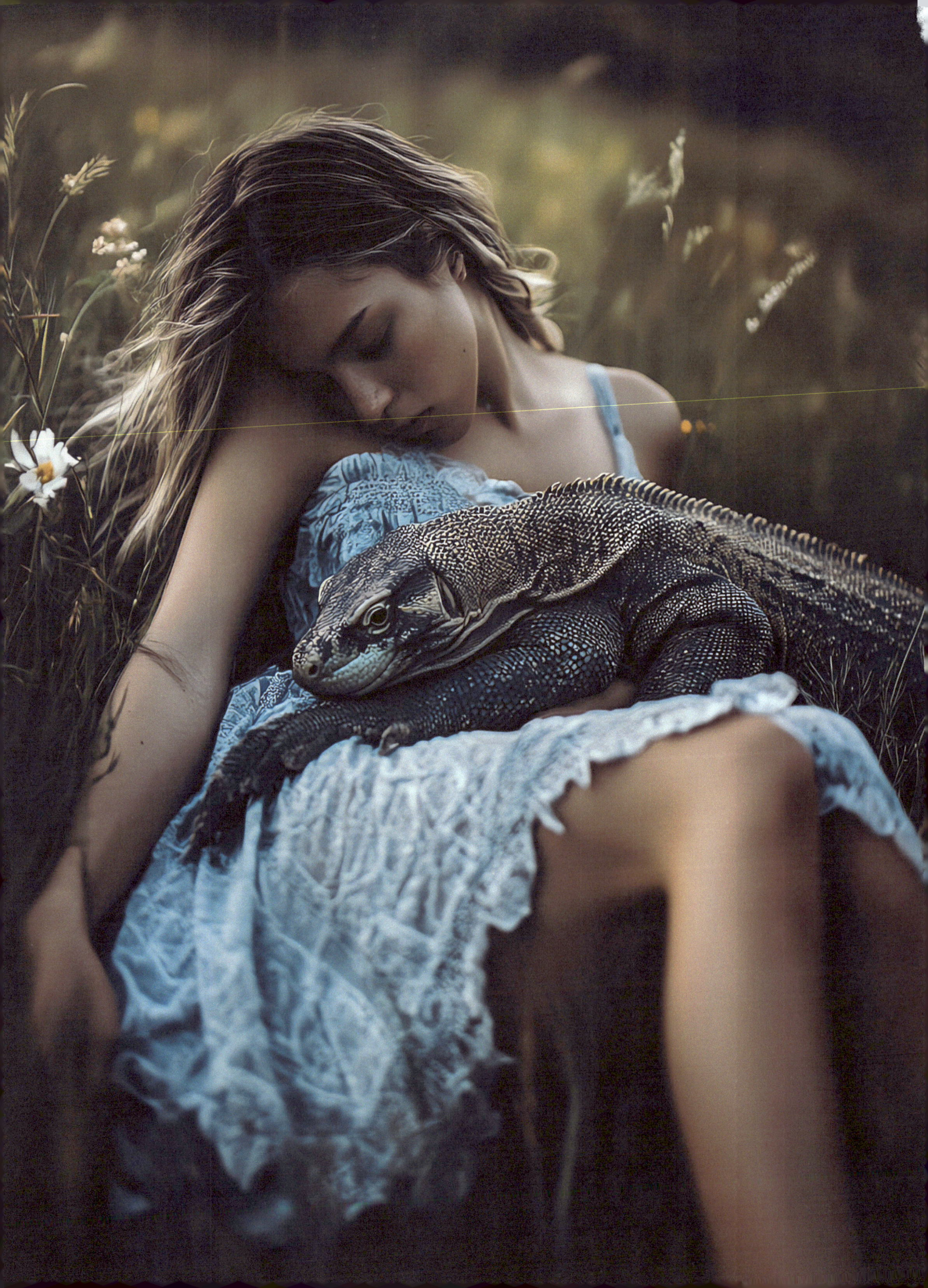

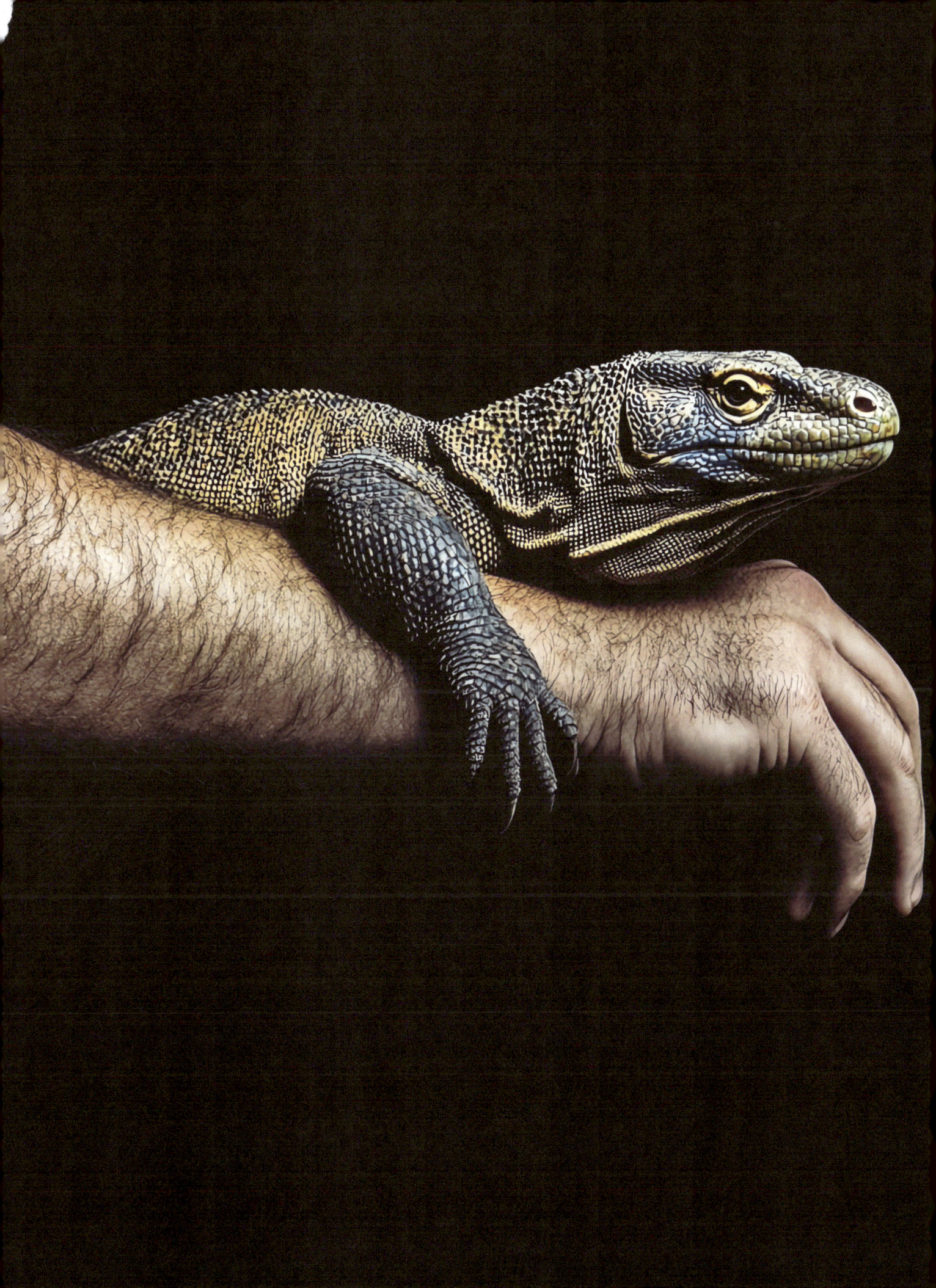

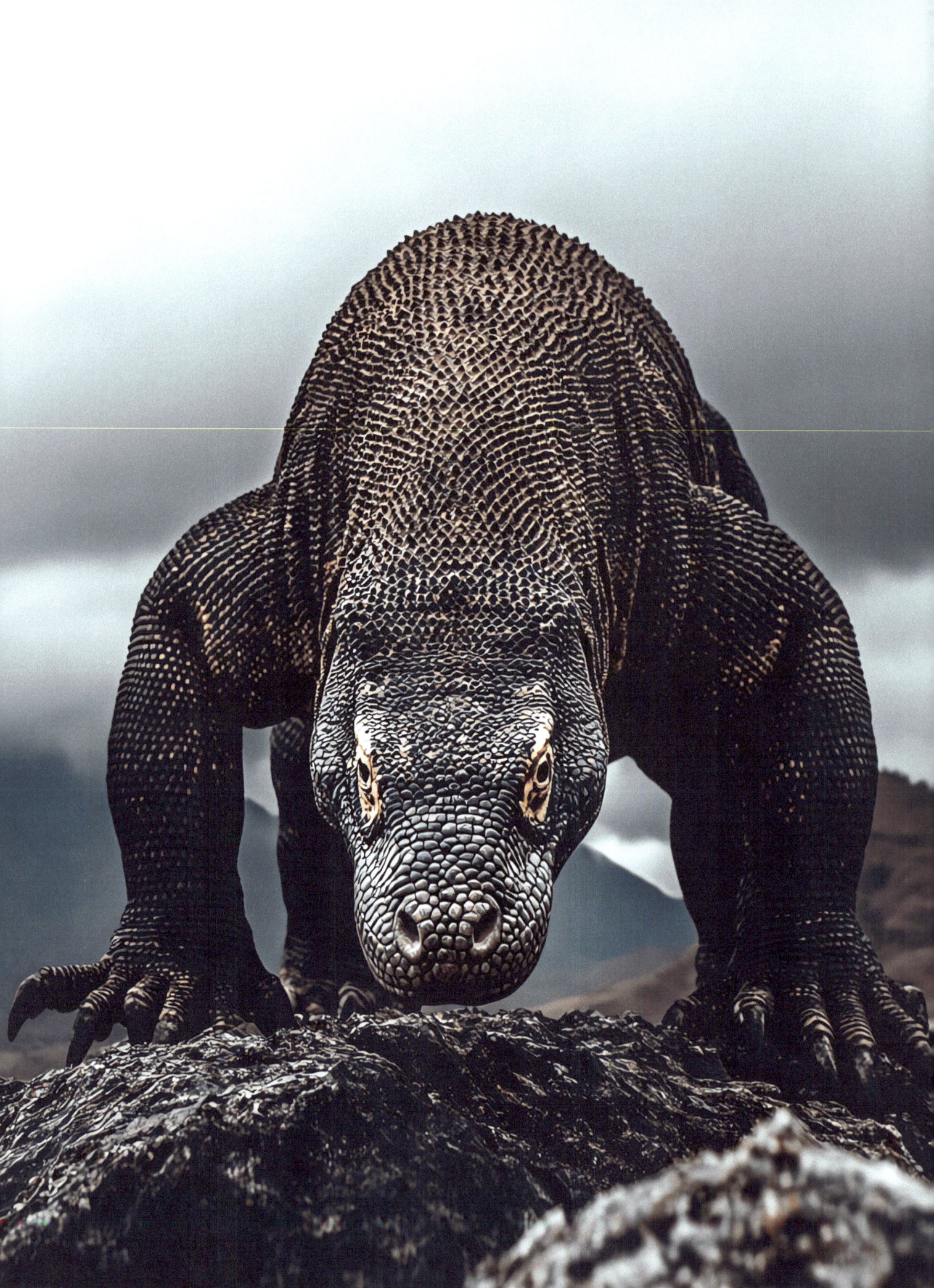

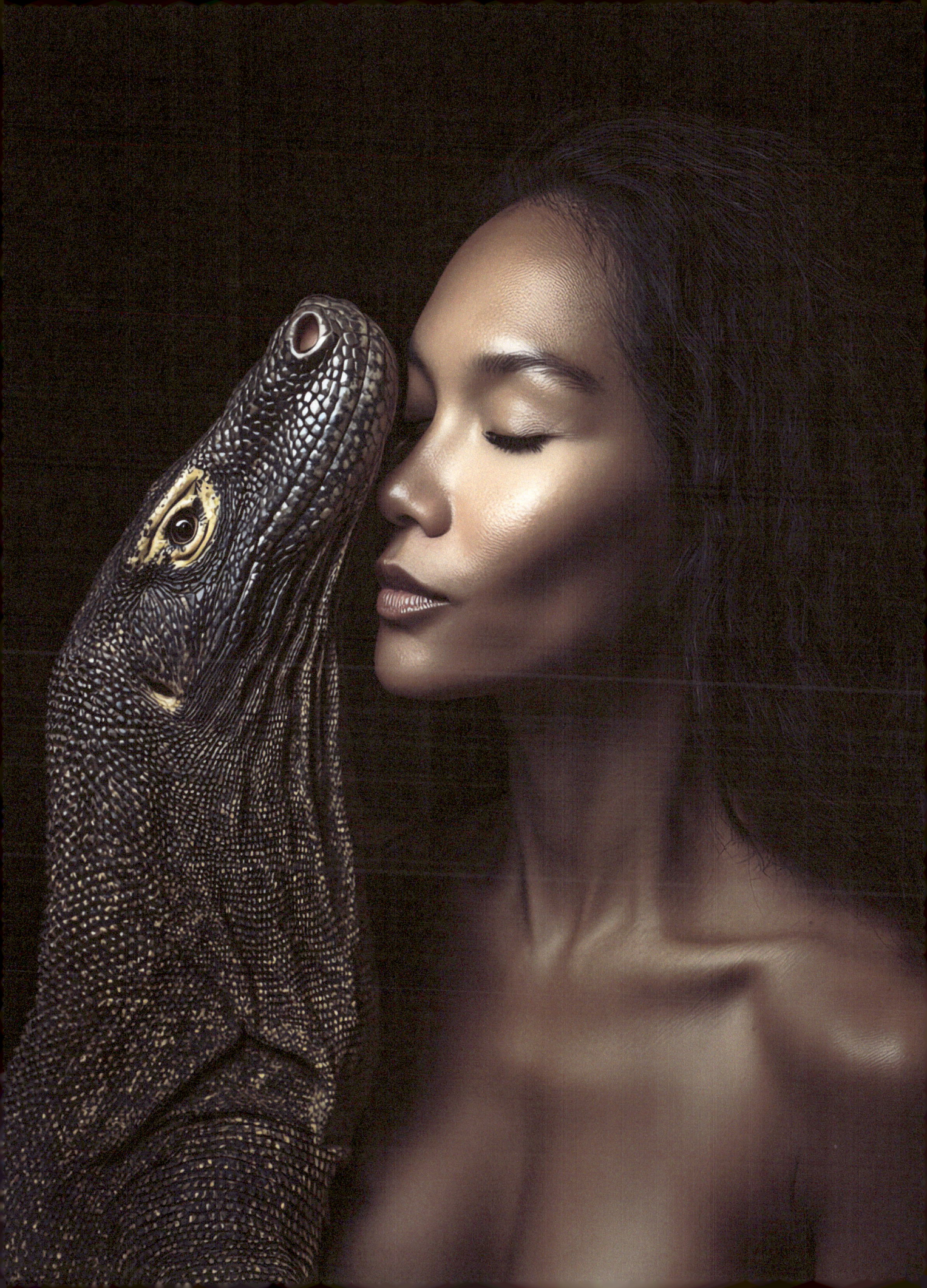

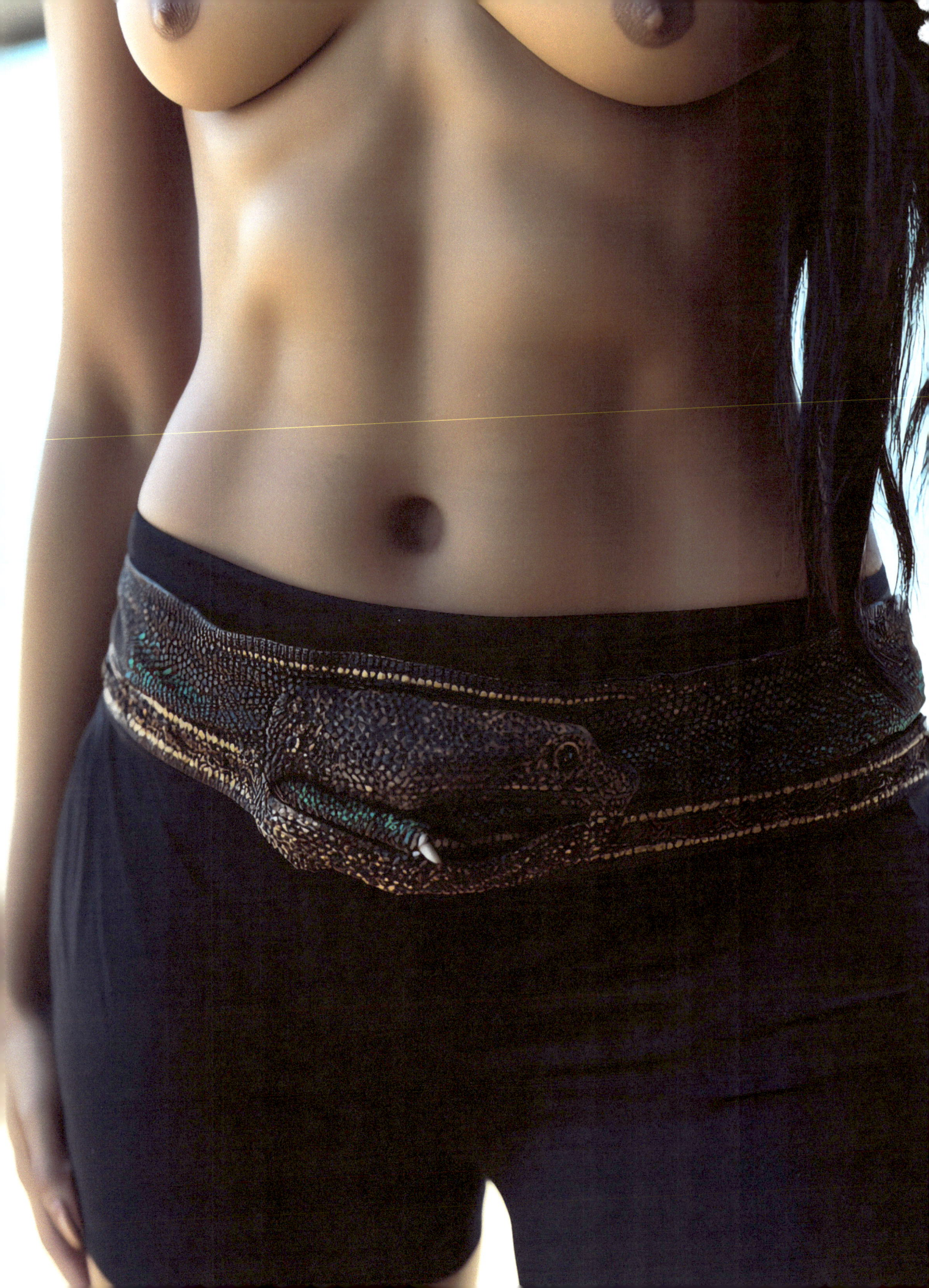

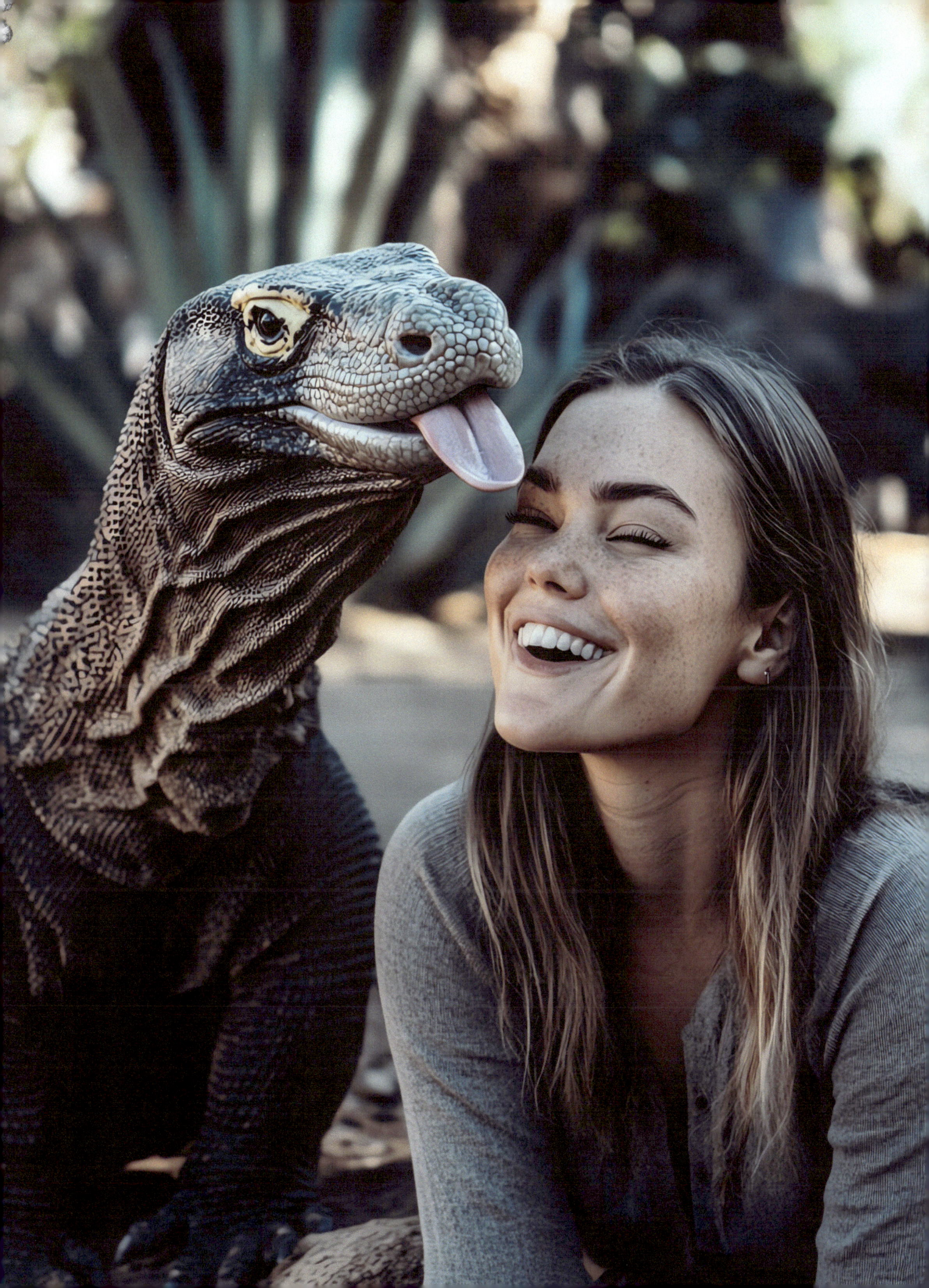

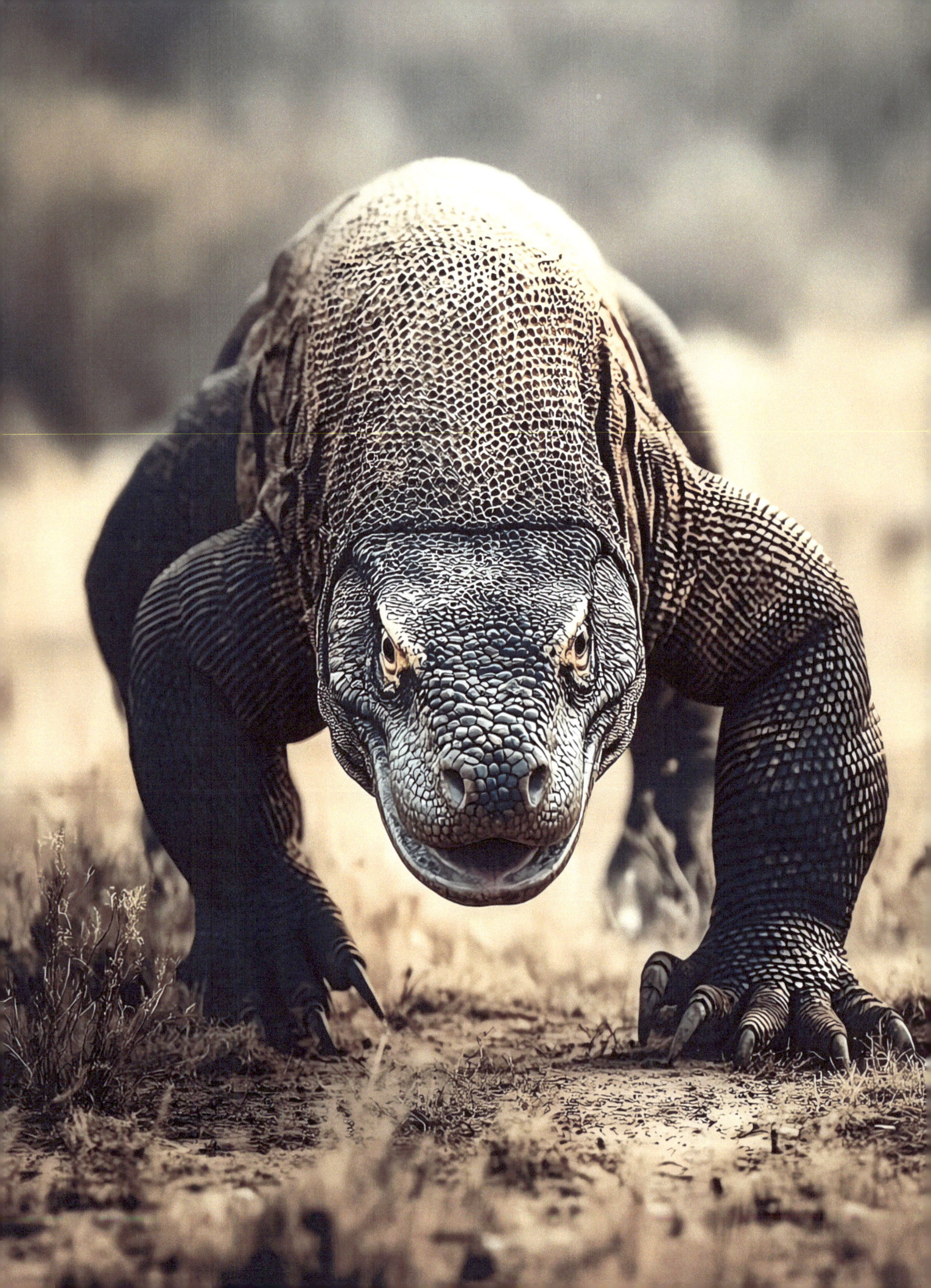

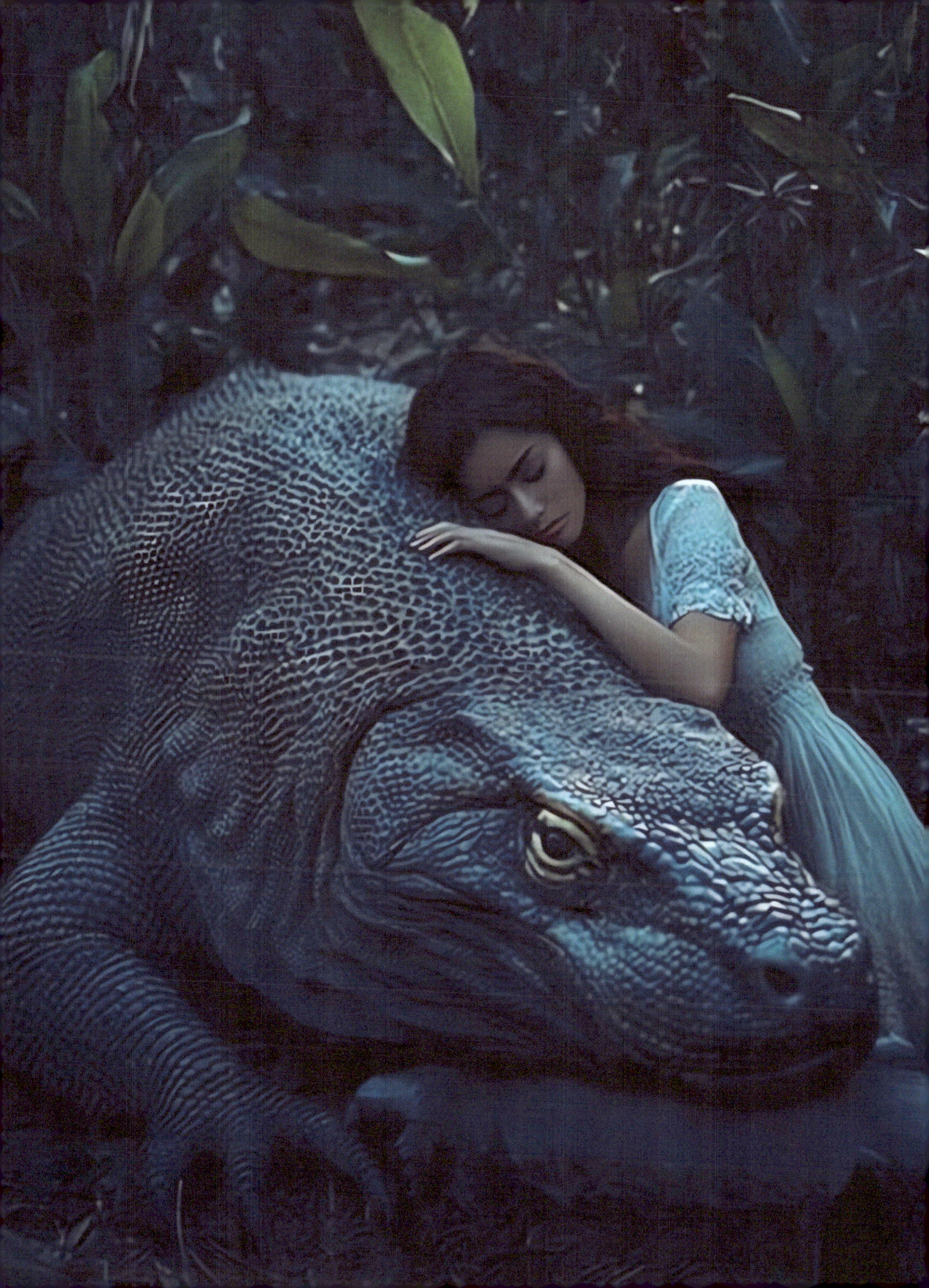

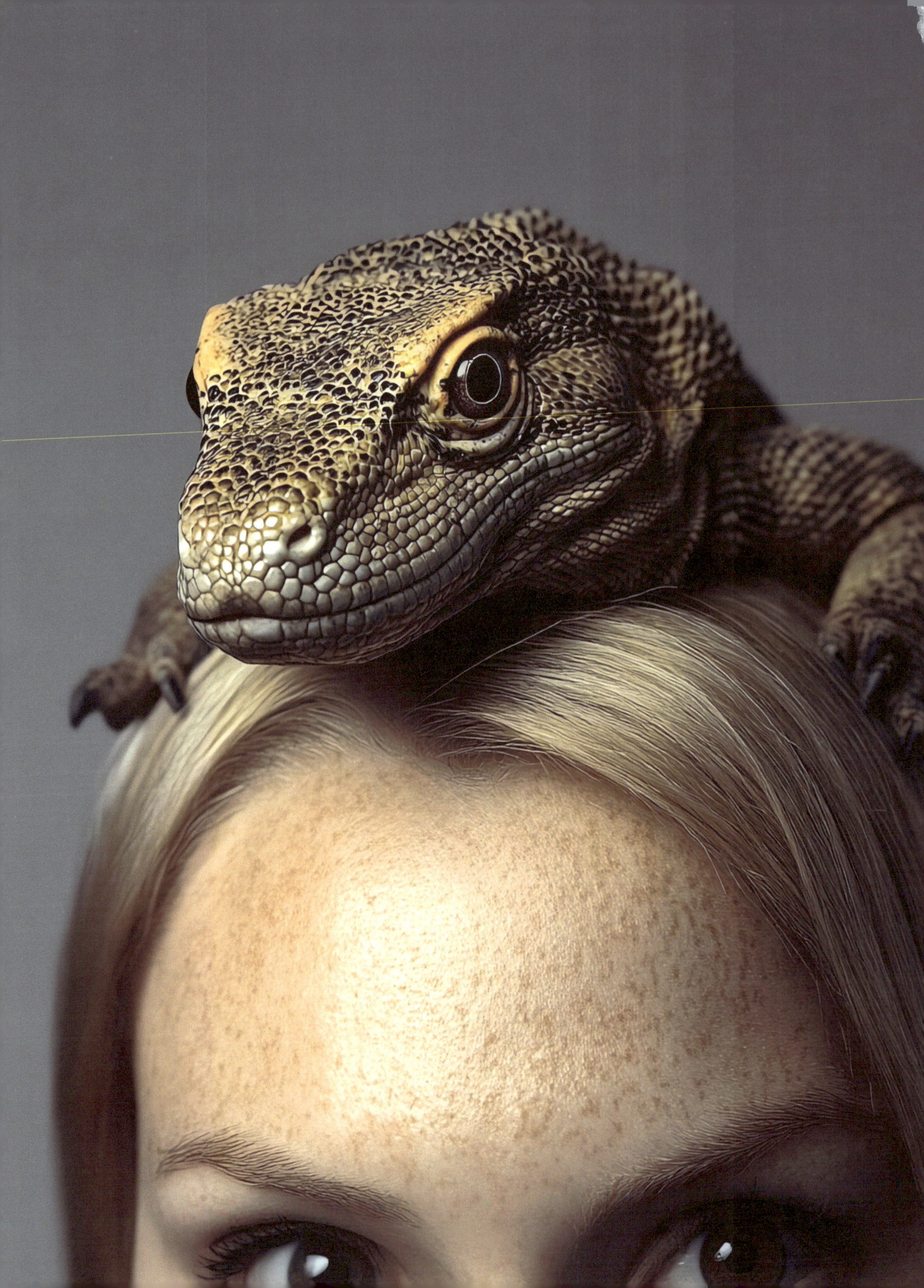

www.ingramcontent.com/pod-product-compliance
Lightning Source LLC
Chambersburg PA
CBHW040438220526
45473CB00004B/1470

1. **Radio Waves**: The longest RF waves, radio waves are commonly used for AM and FM radio, television broadcasts, and even walkie-talkies. These waves are best suited for long-distance transmission because of their ability to travel through the atmosphere and around obstacles.
2. **Microwaves**: Slightly shorter than radio waves, microwaves are used for point-to-point communication, satellite links, and radar. Microwaves are also the key element behind the operation of your microwave oven, where they excite water molecules in food to generate heat.
3. **Infrared Radiation**: Infrared waves have shorter wavelengths and are typically used for remote controls, short-range communication, and thermal imaging. They are also used for security systems and are a part of technologies like infrared night vision cameras.

Although these types of RF waves differ in their specific uses, all of them share a common property: they travel through the air, which makes them incredibly versatile in communication technologies. Yet, this also raises the question: if RF waves are everywhere, can they be blocked or shielded?

The Pervasive Nature of RF Waves in Everyday Life

The influence of RF waves in our lives cannot be overstated. Every day, we interact with numerous devices that rely on RF communication. From the smartphones we carry, to the wireless networks we connect to, to the radio and television broadcasts we enjoy— RF waves are the silent enablers behind the scenes.

In our homes, RF waves emanate from Wi-Fi routers, Bluetooth devices, smart home systems, baby monitors, and even microwave ovens. At work, they power our cellphones, laptops, and wireless office equipment. When we travel, RF waves connect us to satellite GPS systems, cellular networks, and airplane communication systems.

This ever-present connectivity offers tremendous convenience, but it also raises significant concerns about exposure to these electromagnetic fields. The more we rely on RF technologies, the more we are constantly surrounded by these waves—whether we're aware of them or not.

Why Blocking RF Waves is Important

Blocking RF waves has become a growing concern for many reasons. There are three primary considerations: health, privacy, and security.

1. **Health Implications**: Despite widespread belief that RF waves are harmless, there is ongoing debate in the scientific community about their potential health risks. Some studies suggest that prolonged exposure to RF radiation could have adverse effects, particularly with regard to brain health, sleep disruption, and potential links to cancer. Children, whose developing bodies are more sensitive, may face heightened risks, which has led to increased concern from health organizations worldwide.

2. **Privacy Concerns**: RF waves are susceptible to interception, and this creates a significant privacy issue. Hackers can exploit RF signals to intercept phone calls, access personal data, or even spy on individuals. With the growing sophistication of RF-based hacking tools, the need for strong RF blocking methods becomes even more critical.

3. **Security Risks**: In addition to privacy breaches, RF signals also play a role in security vulnerabilities. Hackers and malicious actors can use RF jamming or spoofing techniques to disable communication systems or deceive devices. This can disrupt everything from cell networks to critical infrastructure, leading to a rising concern over the security of our RF-powered world.

As our society becomes increasingly connected, the question of how to shield ourselves from potential risks grows more pressing. The ability to block, shield, or otherwise control exposure to RF waves offers a solution that balances the benefits of modern connectivity with the need for protection.

The Health, Privacy, and Security Implications of RF Exposure

The health risks associated with RF exposure have become a point of ongoing research and debate. Some studies have suggested potential links between prolonged RF exposure and adverse health effects, including increased risk of certain cancers, neurological disorders, and sleep disturbances. While many of these studies are still inconclusive, the possibility that RF radiation could have long-term effects on our health is an issue that warrants further investigation.

The World Health Organization (WHO) and various national health organizations have established guidelines on RF exposure limits, but the debate remains. Most current guidelines set a threshold for exposure based on known effects at higher power levels. However, less is known about the cumulative effects of lower, constant exposure—which is what we experience in our daily lives. This uncertainty prompts many individuals to take proactive measures to shield themselves from RF exposure.

From a privacy and security perspective, the ability of RF signals to travel long distances and penetrate physical barriers means that your personal data is at risk of being intercepted. When you make a call or send data over Wi-Fi, your information can be intercepted by malicious actors with the right tools. This makes RF-blocking technology an essential tool in safeguarding sensitive communications from prying eyes.

Finally, there's the matter of security. The rise of RF-based hacking techniques, such as signal jamming or spoofing, means that an individual's security can be compromised without them even being aware. Jamming disrupts communication by overpowering signals, rendering devices useless, while spoofing tricks devices into connecting to fraudulent sources, such as a fake Wi-Fi network. These threats, while less commonly recognized, are real and pose serious risks to individuals, businesses, and governments.

Conclusion

As we become more interconnected, the need to understand and manage RF exposure has never been more critical. This book will guide you through the various methods of blocking RF waves, exploring the technologies, materials, and strategies that can help protect your health, privacy, and security. We'll delve into the science of RF waves, examine their impact on our lives, and provide practical solutions for minimizing exposure to these pervasive forces. The goal is not to disconnect entirely but to regain control—empowering you to live a healthier, safer, and more secure life in a world of constant RF communication.

In the following chapters, we will explore the electromagnetic spectrum, understand the technologies that rely on RF waves, and learn how to block or shield ourselves from these invisible forces. By the end of this book, you will be equipped with the knowledge and tools to take charge of your exposure to RF radiation and lead a more balanced, protected life.

Chapter 2: Fundamentals of Electromagnetic Waves

Electromagnetic Spectrum Overview

Radio Frequency (RF) waves are a subset of a broader class of energy called electromagnetic waves. These waves make up the **electromagnetic spectrum**, which spans a wide range of frequencies and wavelengths, each with different properties and uses. The spectrum includes everything from extremely low-frequency waves (like the ones used for submarine communication) to extremely high-frequency waves, like gamma rays, which are used in nuclear radiation.

The electromagnetic spectrum is traditionally divided into several categories based on the frequency of the waves. The **lowest frequency** waves, such as **radio waves**, have the longest wavelengths and are used for broadcast communication, like AM and FM radio. The **higher frequency** waves, such as **microwaves** and **infrared**, are used for communications in more focused applications, such as Wi-Fi, Bluetooth, and satellite communications.

The electromagnetic spectrum can be divided into the following key regions (from low to high frequency):

1. **Extremely Low Frequency (ELF)**: 3 Hz to 30 Hz
2. **Very Low Frequency (VLF)**: 30 Hz to 300 Hz
3. **Low Frequency (LF)**: 300 Hz to 3 kHz
4. **Medium Frequency (MF)**: 3 kHz to 30 kHz
5. **High Frequency (HF)**: 30 kHz to 300 kHz
6. **Very High Frequency (VHF)**: 30 MHz to 300 MHz
7. **Ultra High Frequency (UHF)**: 300 MHz to 3 GHz
8. **Super High Frequency (SHF)**: 3 GHz to 30 GHz
9. **Extremely High Frequency (EHF)**: 30 GHz to 300 GHz

RF waves fall into the UHF, SHF, and EHF bands, and they include many types of communication technologies, such as **cellular networks**, **Wi-Fi**, and **microwave communications**.

Radio Waves, Microwaves, and Their Frequencies

The term "radio frequency" specifically refers to electromagnetic waves that fall within the RF portion of the electromagnetic spectrum, generally within the range of **30 Hz to 300 GHz**. Within this range, different types of RF waves have distinct characteristics and uses.

1. **Radio Waves** (3 Hz to 300 MHz)

   These waves are used for communication over long distances. They have the ability to travel great distances through the atmosphere, making them ideal for radio, television broadcasts, and other forms of communication like AM and FM radio, as well as communication with satellites.

2. **Microwaves** (300 MHz to 300 GHz)

   These waves are widely used for **cellular communication**, **radar systems**, and **satellite transmissions**. Microwaves are characterized by their ability to carry large amounts of data, which is why they are used in both consumer technology (like microwave ovens) and advanced communication systems (such as **5G networks**).

3. **Millimeter Waves** (30 GHz to 300 GHz)

   These waves are much shorter in wavelength and are typically used in applications that require high data transmission, such as advanced **wireless networks** (e.g., **5G**). Their high-frequency nature allows them to transmit large amounts of data but also means they have a limited range and are more easily blocked by obstacles.

The **frequency** of these waves directly influences their **propagation characteristics**—lower frequency waves, like those used in AM radio, can travel long distances, often bouncing off the ionosphere, while higher-frequency waves, such as those used for Wi-Fi or microwave ovens, have a shorter range but can carry more data and operate at higher speeds.

Understanding the Physics Behind RF Waves

At the core of **RF communication** lies the **physics of electromagnetic radiation**. RF waves are a type of electromagnetic wave, which is a disturbance in the electromagnetic field that propagates through space. These waves carry energy and can move through the vacuum of space as well as through mediums like air, water, or solids.

Electromagnetic waves are created when **charged particles**, such as electrons, oscillate and generate a magnetic field that induces an electric field, and vice versa. This oscillation is what creates the characteristic wave pattern of electromagnetic radiation. The speed at which these waves travel is a constant in a vacuum, at approximately **3×10^8 meters per second** (the speed of light).

The **wavelength** of an electromagnetic wave is inversely related to its **frequency**. As frequency increases, wavelength decreases, meaning that high-frequency waves, such as microwaves, have shorter wavelengths than low-frequency radio waves. The wavelength and frequency together determine the wave's energy: high-frequency waves carry more energy, which is why they are used in powerful communication systems and technologies.

In practical terms, RF waves interact with materials in a variety of ways. Some materials, such as metals, can reflect or absorb RF waves, while others, like air or glass, allow them to pass through with varying degrees of resistance. This is why understanding how RF waves propagate is essential in both designing communication systems and shielding against unwanted exposure.

The Impact of RF on Human Health and the Environment

The potential health effects of RF exposure have been a subject of scientific study for decades. As wireless technologies have become more widespread, particularly with the rise of mobile phones, Wi-Fi, and 5G networks, concerns have increased about the long-term exposure to RF waves and their potential biological effects.

1. **Thermal Effects**

   One well-understood effect of RF radiation is its ability to generate heat when absorbed by body tissues. This is the same principle used in **microwave ovens**, where microwaves excite water molecules in food to generate heat. However, when the body absorbs RF energy, it can also lead to tissue heating. This is generally a concern only at very high exposure levels, such as those experienced during the operation of certain industrial equipment.

2. **Non-Thermal Effects**

   There has been growing interest in the potential non-thermal effects of RF exposure—effects that occur at levels of RF radiation that are too low to cause noticeable heating. Studies suggest that long-term exposure to RF waves could potentially affect biological processes at the cellular level, such as DNA damage or altered cell function. However, conclusive evidence linking non-thermal RF exposure to serious health effects, such as cancer or neurological disorders, remains limited.

3. **Environmental Concerns**

In addition to human health risks, there are concerns about the environmental impact of widespread RF usage. While RF waves do not have the same biological effects on plants or animals as they do on humans, large-scale RF exposure—such as the operation of numerous cell towers or satellite systems—could impact ecosystems in subtle ways. Some studies suggest that animals, especially those with sensitive biological systems like birds and bees, might be affected by RF radiation, but the scientific consensus is still emerging.

Scientific Studies on RF Wave Exposure

Over the past few decades, a number of studies have been conducted to understand the potential risks of RF exposure. Key areas of focus in these studies include:

- **Cellular Effects**: The effects of RF on human cells and tissues are among the most extensively studied. Research has looked into whether RF exposure leads to mutations, cell damage, or an increased risk of cancers such as brain tumors. While most studies have found no conclusive evidence linking RF exposure to these effects, a small number of studies have raised concerns about the possibility of low-level RF exposure over long periods.

- **Neurological Effects**: Another area of research focuses on how RF waves might affect the brain and central nervous system. There is some evidence suggesting that exposure to RF radiation can alter brain function, including effects on sleep patterns, cognitive performance, and emotional regulation. However, these studies remain inconclusive and more research is needed to fully understand the long-term neurological effects of RF exposure.

- **Epidemiological Studies**: Large-scale epidemiological studies have sought to establish a link between RF exposure from mobile phones and other sources and various health outcomes. While the majority of these studies have failed to show a direct link between RF exposure and health problems, the rapid growth of mobile phone use, particularly among young people, has led some researchers to call for more targeted studies on potential long-term effects.

As technology continues to evolve, more research is needed to fully understand the complex relationship between RF exposure and human health. This underscores the importance of being mindful of our exposure to RF waves and seeking ways to minimize potential risks.

Conclusion

Understanding the fundamentals of electromagnetic waves, particularly RF waves, is crucial in navigating the world of wireless communication. The electromagnetic spectrum governs the propagation of RF waves, and the physics behind them determines how they interact with various materials and living organisms. While the impact of RF exposure on human health is still a subject of scientific debate, it is clear that understanding these waves and how to shield ourselves from excessive exposure is increasingly important. As wireless communication becomes more integral to our lives, mastering the art of disconnecting from RF waves will be essential for maintaining both our well-being and privacy in an interconnected world.

Chapter 3: RF Communication Technologies

In today's digital age, we are surrounded by a multitude of devices that depend on Radio Frequency (RF) communication. From smartphones to Wi-Fi routers, and even satellite systems, RF technologies power nearly all forms of wireless communication. This chapter will explore the key RF communication devices, how they work, and the infrastructure that supports their use. Understanding these technologies is crucial to mastering the art of disconnecting from RF waves and shielding yourself from potential health, privacy, and security risks.

Types of Communication Devices

RF communication is the backbone of many essential devices that are part of our daily lives. These devices use RF signals to transmit and receive data, facilitating everything from personal communication to global positioning systems. The most common types of RF communication devices include:

1. Cellphones and Smartphones

Cellphones are perhaps the most ubiquitous RF devices in the modern world. These devices use RF waves to communicate with cell towers, which provide the infrastructure for mobile networks like 4G, 5G, and beyond. Smartphones are more than just voice communication tools; they also rely on RF for text messages, mobile internet, GPS, and Bluetooth. The RF signals used by smartphones typically operate in the **UHF (Ultra High Frequency)** and **SHF (Super High Frequency)** bands, enabling them to send and receive large amounts of data at high speeds.

2. Wi-Fi Networks

Wi-Fi, a popular method of accessing the internet wirelessly, uses RF waves to transmit data between devices like laptops, smartphones, and wireless routers. Wi-Fi typically operates in the **2.4 GHz** and **5 GHz** bands, with the newer **Wi-Fi 6** technologies expanding into even higher frequency bands. The frequency and range of these RF waves make Wi-Fi a highly effective solution for providing internet access over short distances, such as within homes, offices, and public spaces.

3. Bluetooth Devices

Bluetooth is another RF communication technology used for short-range data exchange, most commonly between personal devices like headphones, smartwatches, and speakers. Operating in the **2.4 GHz** frequency range, Bluetooth uses low power RF signals to connect devices over relatively short distances, typically up to 100 meters. It's designed for low energy consumption, which makes it ideal for battery-powered devices.

4. Satellite Communication Systems

Satellites rely on RF waves to communicate with ground stations and other satellites in orbit. These systems are vital for global communications, television broadcasting, weather monitoring, and GPS services. Satellites use a range of RF frequencies, from the **L-band** (1-2 GHz) for GPS signals to the **Ku-band** and **Ka-band** (12-40 GHz) for broadband communication.

5. Radio and Television Broadcasting

Traditional radio and television broadcasting rely heavily on RF waves to transmit audio and video signals over long distances. Radio stations typically broadcast in the **AM** (Amplitude Modulation) and **FM** (Frequency Modulation) bands, while TV stations use similar RF bands to send high-definition video and sound signals. Although these technologies are being supplanted by digital and streaming media, they are still significant sources of RF radiation in many regions.

6. Radars

Radar systems, used for navigation, weather monitoring, and military applications, also depend on RF waves. Radar works by emitting RF signals and measuring the time it takes for them to bounce back after hitting an object, thus providing information about distance, speed, and direction. Military radar systems can operate at frequencies ranging from **1 GHz to 100 GHz**, depending on their purpose.

How These Devices Transmit and Receive Signals

The process of RF communication involves several steps: transmitting, traveling through space, and receiving the signal. The basic operation of RF devices relies on the same fundamental principle of **modulating** a carrier wave (the RF signal) to carry data. This can be done through various methods, such as **amplitude modulation** (AM), **frequency modulation** (FM), or **phase modulation** (PM).

1. Transmission

For a device like a smartphone or router to transmit data, it first generates an electrical signal that is then converted into an RF signal by an **oscillator**. This RF signal is transmitted by an **antenna**, which sends the waves out into the surrounding environment. The signal is modulated to encode information, such as voice data, internet packets, or video content, which are then sent to the receiving device.

2. Propagation

Once the RF signal leaves the transmitting device, it travels through the air (or space, in the case of satellites) until it reaches the receiving device. The signal can travel through different mediums, such as air, glass, or metal, but the efficiency of transmission depends on factors like **distance**, **frequency**, **obstacles**, and **interference**. Lower-frequency waves (like those used in AM radio) can travel long distances, even bouncing off the ionosphere, while higher-frequency waves (like microwaves and millimeter waves) are more limited in range and can be blocked by obstacles such as walls or trees.

3. Reception

On the receiving end, an antenna picks up the RF signal, which is then fed to a **receiver**. The receiver demodulates the signal, extracting the data encoded in the carrier wave. This data is then processed and presented to the user, such as displaying an internet page, playing a video, or producing sound from a radio.

The Role of Satellites and Towers in RF Communication

Satellites and communication towers play an indispensable role in RF communication. These structures provide the physical infrastructure that supports long-range RF transmission.

1. Cell Towers

Cell towers are part of the cellular network infrastructure, allowing mobile phones to connect to the network. These towers are equipped with antennas that receive RF signals from nearby devices and transmit them to other towers or back to central servers. Each tower operates within a specific **cell** in a network, ensuring that calls and data can be routed to the correct location. The **macrocell towers** provide coverage over large areas, while **small cells** and **microcells** help improve signal strength in urban environments or other areas with high demand.

2. Satellite Communication

Satellites in **geostationary orbit** (about 35,786 km above the Earth) are used for long-range communication, as they provide a clear line of sight to large portions of the Earth's surface. Satellites are equipped with RF transponders that transmit and receive RF signals to ground stations or other satellites. Some satellites, such as those used for **GPS**, provide highly accurate positioning data, while others, like **weather satellites**, use RF signals to capture atmospheric data. The **low Earth orbit (LEO)** and **medium Earth orbit (MEO)** satellites are used for high-speed data transfer and internet services.

The Infrastructure That Supports RF Communication

The infrastructure behind RF communication is vast, complex, and global. In addition to towers and satellites, it includes cables, fiber-optic networks, and data centers that handle the data routing and processing. In a mobile phone system, for example, the signal travels from the phone to a nearby cell tower, then to a central switching station, and finally to the recipient's device, whether it's another mobile phone or a landline. Similarly, Wi-Fi signals typically travel through routers connected to high-speed fiber-optic lines, which connect to the broader internet backbone.

Conclusion

RF communication technologies are the invisible engines that power much of our modern world. From cellphones and Wi-Fi networks to satellite systems and radio broadcasts, RF waves enable us to stay connected, communicate, and access information on a global scale. Understanding the devices and infrastructure that rely on RF waves is the first step in learning how to shield yourself from potential risks. Whether it's managing your exposure to cell tower signals or controlling your Wi-Fi network at home, the next chapters will explore how you can take charge of your interaction with RF technology and its effects on your health, privacy, and security.

Chapter 4: Health Impacts of RF Waves

As wireless technologies continue to permeate every aspect of our lives, concerns about the potential health impacts of prolonged exposure to Radio Frequency (RF) waves have emerged. While we benefit from enhanced connectivity and modern communication, questions about the long-term effects of RF exposure remain at the forefront of public health discussions. This chapter explores the short-term and long-term health impacts of RF waves, the psychological and physiological effects, the ongoing research and debates, and the potential impact on children, the elderly, and sensitive individuals.

Short-term vs Long-term Effects of RF Exposure

The health effects of RF waves can be divided into **short-term** and **long-term** impacts, though much of the research has focused on potential long-term consequences.

Short-term Effects

The short-term effects of RF exposure are often related to **thermal effects**—meaning the heating of tissues. This is a well-understood phenomenon, as RF waves, especially those in the microwave range, can generate heat. For instance, when RF energy is absorbed by the human body, it causes the tissue to warm, which is the same principle used in microwave ovens to heat food. However, at low levels of exposure, the body is capable of dissipating this heat without harm. Short-term exposure to RF radiation at safe levels typically does not lead to significant health issues.

In daily life, most RF exposure, like that from cellphones, Wi-Fi, and Bluetooth, is at low levels and does not cause noticeable heating. Consequently, short-term effects such as **fatigue** or **headaches** are often reported but are typically minor and fleeting. However, the impact on specific individuals may vary depending on the intensity of exposure and the length of time spent in an RF environment.

Long-term Effects

The long-term health effects of RF exposure are much more contentious and remain a topic of extensive research. Prolonged exposure to RF radiation has been linked to various concerns, particularly with devices like cellphones, which are held close to the head and emit RF waves over extended periods.

1. **Cancer Risks**: One of the most significant health concerns associated with long-term RF exposure is its potential to increase the risk of cancer. The **International Agency for Research on Cancer (IARC)**, a part of the World Health Organization (WHO), classifies RF radiation as a **Group 2B carcinogen**—meaning it is possibly carcinogenic to humans, based on an increased risk of glioma, a type of brain cancer. However, studies have yet to establish a clear and definitive link between RF exposure and cancer, and the evidence remains inconclusive.

2. **Neurological Effects**: Other studies suggest that prolonged exposure to RF waves may have neurological consequences. Some individuals have reported experiencing **cognitive effects**, such as memory loss, reduced concentration, or brain fog, when exposed to RF radiation for extended periods. Though there is no conclusive evidence linking RF exposure to neurodegenerative diseases like Alzheimer's or Parkinson's, these concerns continue to be studied in greater depth.

3. **Reproductive Health**: There is ongoing research into whether RF exposure may affect reproductive health. Studies have explored the potential link between RF exposure and **sperm count** or **sperm motility**, with some suggesting that long-term RF exposure could impact male fertility. However, these studies are not conclusive, and further research is needed.

Psychological and Physiological Effects

In addition to the more commonly discussed health risks, RF exposure may also have significant psychological and physiological effects.

Psychological Effects

There is growing interest in the **psychological** impacts of RF exposure. Some studies suggest that RF radiation may be linked to **increased stress**, **anxiety**, and **sleep disturbances**. This phenomenon has been particularly noted in individuals who live in areas with high levels of RF exposure, such as those living near cell towers or individuals who work in environments with high RF activity. Symptoms such as **electrosensitivity** or **electromagnetic hypersensitivity (EHS)** have been reported by some people, where they experience a variety of symptoms such as **headaches**, **tinnitus**, **fatigue**, and **irritability** when exposed to electromagnetic fields.

Despite these reports, the scientific consensus remains divided on whether these symptoms are directly caused by RF exposure or are the result of psychological factors, such as anxiety or a nocebo effect, where people believe they are being harmed by the exposure.

Physiological Effects

Physiologically, exposure to RF radiation may affect different body systems. A few studies suggest that **RF waves** can influence **blood pressure**, **heart rate**, and **hormonal balances**. Long-term exposure could potentially result in **endocrine disruptions**, though these findings are still under scrutiny. In particular, **melatonin production**—a hormone that regulates sleep cycles—has been shown in some studies to decrease in response to RF exposure, leading to concerns about the impact on sleep patterns and circadian rhythms.

Ongoing Research and Debates in the Scientific Community

There is a significant amount of research being conducted globally on the health effects of RF waves. However, the research remains controversial and inconclusive for several reasons:

1. **Study Methodology**: One of the challenges in studying the health effects of RF exposure is the variability in study design. Some studies have focused on **animal models**, while others look at human populations exposed to varying levels of RF. The type, intensity, and duration of exposure all vary across studies, making it difficult to draw definitive conclusions.
2. **Lack of Consensus**: Scientific communities remain divided on the potential risks. While some health organizations, such as the **American Cancer Society** and **National Institutes of Health (NIH)**, assert that there is no conclusive evidence that RF exposure causes harm at levels typically encountered by the public, others, such as the **Environmental Health Trust** and certain independent researchers, caution against underestimating the potential risks.
3. **Cumulative Effects**: Another challenge is the issue of **cumulative exposure**. Modern life involves constant exposure to RF waves—whether through phones, Wi-Fi networks, or various forms of wireless technology. The long-term cumulative impact of this ongoing exposure is still largely unknown, and more studies are needed to determine the potential health consequences of a lifetime spent surrounded by RF radiation.

The Impact on Children, Elderly, and Sensitive Individuals

Certain populations may be more vulnerable to the potential health effects of RF exposure.

1. **Children**: Children are considered more susceptible to the potential effects of RF exposure due to their developing tissues, thinner skulls, and smaller size. Research has shown that RF waves may penetrate the skull more deeply in children than in adults, which raises concerns about the long-term impact on their developing brains. While studies on the direct link between RF exposure and childhood cancer are still inconclusive, many experts recommend taking a cautious approach, particularly when it comes to children using cellphones for long periods.

2. **Elderly**: Older adults may also be more vulnerable to the potential effects of RF exposure due to age-related changes in tissue density and reduced ability to repair cellular damage. Additionally, those who have existing health conditions, such as **neurological disorders, cancer,** or **cardiovascular disease**, may be at higher risk of experiencing exacerbated health effects from RF exposure.

3. **Electrosensitive Individuals**: Some individuals report heightened sensitivity to electromagnetic fields, a condition referred to as **electromagnetic hypersensitivity (EHS)**. While this condition is not officially recognized as a medical diagnosis, these individuals may experience symptoms like headaches, fatigue, dizziness, or skin irritation when exposed to RF radiation. Research on EHS remains inconclusive, but for these individuals, even low-level RF exposure may be more harmful than for others.

Conclusion

The potential health impacts of RF waves remain a highly debated topic in the scientific community. While there is no conclusive evidence linking everyday levels of RF exposure to significant health problems, ongoing research continues to explore the long-term risks associated with prolonged exposure. Given the rapid increase in RF-emitting devices and technologies, it is essential to take a precautionary approach—especially for vulnerable populations like children, the elderly, and those with electrosensitivity. As more studies are conducted, we may gain a clearer understanding of the true impact of RF radiation on human health, allowing us to make informed decisions about managing our exposure in a world increasingly dependent on wireless communication.

Chapter 5: Security Concerns with RF Signals

Radio Frequency (RF) waves are the invisible threads that connect our modern world. While they provide the foundation for numerous communication technologies, they also open doors for security vulnerabilities. As we become increasingly dependent on wireless communication, the risks of RF-based attacks have risen, threatening our privacy, data integrity, and even our physical security. This chapter will explore the various ways RF signals can be intercepted, discuss common RF-based hacking techniques, examine the vulnerabilities of modern communication systems, and offer strategies to protect your privacy in an RF-powered world.

How RF Signals Can Be Intercepted

RF signals are the key to wireless communication, but their very nature also makes them inherently vulnerable. Unlike wired communication, which is contained within a physical medium, RF signals travel through the air, meaning they can be intercepted by anyone with the right equipment.

1. **Broadcasting Nature**: RF signals, by their nature, are not confined to a specific device or space. A wireless router, for example, broadcasts Wi-Fi signals that can be detected by any nearby device capable of receiving the signal. This makes it easier for malicious actors to tap into networks, intercept communications, and potentially gain unauthorized access to private data.

2. **Line-of-Sight Propagation**: Many RF signals, especially those used in satellite communication and radar systems, rely on a line-of-sight pathway. While this generally ensures a direct connection between sender and receiver, it also means that signals are more susceptible to interception if they are not properly encrypted or shielded, especially over long distances.

3. **Weak or Unsecured Signals**: Many devices, particularly older models or improperly configured networks, transmit RF signals without any encryption or security protocols. This leaves them vulnerable to interception by hackers who can listen in on conversations or extract sensitive data. Even signals that are encrypted can be intercepted and analyzed if the encryption keys are weak or compromised.

Examples of RF-based Hacking Techniques

The ability to intercept and manipulate RF signals has led to the development of various hacking techniques. These methods exploit the vulnerabilities inherent in wireless communication systems and can have serious consequences for individuals, businesses, and even governments. Some common RF-based hacking techniques include:

1. Man-in-the-Middle Attacks

In a **man-in-the-middle (MITM)** attack, the hacker intercepts and potentially alters the communication between two parties without their knowledge. For example, when a user connects to an unsecured Wi-Fi network, an attacker can position themselves between the user and the network, intercepting data such as passwords, credit card information, or personal emails. MITM attacks can also occur in Bluetooth and cellular networks, where hackers can intercept data being sent between devices.

2. RF Jamming

RF jamming involves transmitting powerful RF signals that interfere with legitimate communication systems. By overwhelming a frequency with noise, attackers can disable wireless networks, GPS systems, or even prevent communications between essential infrastructure components, such as military or emergency services. This can have severe consequences in areas like air traffic control, military operations, and communication in critical situations.

3. Spoofing

Spoofing is another RF-based hacking technique in which an attacker impersonates a legitimate device or communication network. For example, a hacker could create a fake Wi-Fi hotspot that mimics a legitimate network. When a user unknowingly connects to the spoofed network, the attacker can intercept their data or even inject malicious software onto the device.

In the case of GPS spoofing, attackers can send out false GPS signals to deceive a device about its actual location. This has been used to mislead navigation systems, affecting everything from civilian vehicles to aircraft.

4. Eavesdropping

Eavesdropping is the act of intercepting and listening in on RF signals to gather sensitive information. With the right tools, attackers can intercept signals from various devices, including radios, phones, and wireless networks. Even encrypted signals can be intercepted and analyzed if the encryption scheme is weak, or if attackers can obtain the decryption keys.

Eavesdropping can be particularly dangerous in environments where sensitive information is transmitted, such as corporate boardrooms, government buildings, or private homes. Attackers can harvest personal details, financial data, or confidential business information simply by listening to unprotected RF signals.

Vulnerabilities of Modern Communication Systems

Despite advances in security technologies, modern communication systems still have significant vulnerabilities, many of which stem from their reliance on RF signals. These vulnerabilities can lead to privacy breaches, data theft, and potential physical threats. Some of the most concerning weaknesses include:

1. Lack of Proper Encryption

While many communication systems use encryption to secure data, not all RF-based communications are encrypted, and some use outdated or weak encryption protocols. Systems like Wi-Fi, Bluetooth, and cellular networks are prime examples of communication technologies that can be vulnerable to interception if not properly secured. Even when encryption is used, hackers may exploit flaws in the encryption algorithm or steal encryption keys to gain access to sensitive data.

2. Over-reliance on Wireless Infrastructure

Many critical infrastructures, such as financial networks, emergency services, and government communication systems, rely heavily on wireless communication. This over-reliance on wireless infrastructure makes them vulnerable to RF attacks, as attackers can exploit weaknesses in the security of these systems. For example, in the event of RF jamming, entire communication networks can be disabled, leading to widespread disruptions in essential services.

3. RF-based Hacking Tools

With the increasing availability of affordable RF hacking tools, such as software-defined radios (SDRs) and portable jammers, the barrier to entry for RF-based hacking has significantly lowered. These tools allow individuals with minimal technical expertise to interfere with or intercept RF signals. This has led to an increase in RF-based attacks, ranging from criminal activities to more sophisticated state-sponsored espionage.

Protecting Your Privacy in an RF-Powered World

While RF signals are inherently vulnerable, there are several strategies you can adopt to protect your privacy and security in an RF-powered world. Implementing effective security measures can help you reduce the risks associated with RF-based hacking and interception.

1. Use Encryption

Encryption is one of the most effective ways to protect your RF communications. Whether you're using a Wi-Fi network, Bluetooth device, or cellular network, make sure that your communications are encrypted. For example, use **WPA3 encryption** for Wi-Fi, and avoid using open or unsecured Wi-Fi networks. For personal devices, such as smartphones, ensure that **end-to-end encryption** is enabled for messaging and communication apps.

2. Avoid Public Wi-Fi Networks

Public Wi-Fi networks are particularly vulnerable to attacks, such as man-in-the-middle attacks and eavesdropping. When using public Wi-Fi, avoid transmitting sensitive information like passwords, banking details, or personal data. If you must connect to a public network, use a **Virtual Private Network (VPN)** to encrypt your connection and protect your data.

3. Use Secure Communication Devices

Investing in secure communication devices is another important step. Look for phones and Wi-Fi routers that offer advanced security features, such as built-in encryption and anti-jamming capabilities. If you're in an environment where sensitive communication is a priority, consider using **encrypted communication services** that offer higher levels of privacy and security.

4. Shield Your Devices

To physically protect your devices from RF interception, consider using **Faraday bags** or **RF-blocking cases** for sensitive equipment like phones, laptops, and credit cards. These shields block external RF signals from reaching your device, reducing the likelihood of interception or tracking. Faraday cages can also be used to block signals in specific areas, such as offices or homes, to protect against unauthorized surveillance.

5. Educate Yourself and Stay Vigilant

Staying informed about the latest security threats and best practices for protecting your RF communications is essential. Regularly update your devices with the latest security patches, use strong passwords, and avoid clicking on suspicious links or downloading untrusted files. The more vigilant you are, the better you can safeguard your privacy in a world of RF-powered communication.

Conclusion

RF signals play an essential role in modern communication, but their open nature also exposes us to a range of security risks. From interception and eavesdropping to more sophisticated attacks like RF jamming and spoofing, the vulnerabilities of RF-based systems are a growing concern. However, by understanding these risks and adopting the proper security measures—such as encryption, device shielding, and careful use of public networks—you can protect your privacy and reduce the likelihood of falling victim to RF-based attacks. As we continue to rely on wireless communication in every aspect of our lives, mastering the art of protecting our RF-powered communications will be essential for safeguarding our digital lives.

Chapter 6: Introduction to RF Blocking

As the prevalence of wireless communication technologies continues to expand, so too does the importance of understanding how to manage and block Radio Frequency (RF) waves. Blocking RF waves is no longer just a concern for those worried about privacy or health; it's becoming an essential practice for protecting personal data, safeguarding health, and reducing unwanted interference. In this chapter, we will explore the concept of **RF blocking and shielding**, the materials commonly used to block RF signals, the benefits and challenges associated with blocking RF waves, and the legal and ethical considerations surrounding RF shielding.

The Concept of RF Blocking and Shielding

RF blocking, or shielding, refers to the practice of using materials and technologies designed to prevent RF waves from passing through or interfering with a specific environment. Whether the goal is to protect personal health, secure communication networks, or create isolated zones for certain activities, RF blocking can be an effective way to control exposure to RF radiation.

RF shielding works by either reflecting or absorbing the energy from RF signals. The primary principle behind blocking RF waves is that materials with conductive properties (like metals) or absorbent properties (like special fabrics) can disrupt or block the path of electromagnetic waves. The effectiveness of shielding depends on various factors, including the frequency of the RF signals, the material properties of the shield, and the thickness or coverage of the shielding.

In simpler terms, RF blocking ensures that RF signals do not interfere with critical communications or inadvertently expose individuals to potentially harmful radiation.

Materials Used for RF Wave Blocking

To effectively block RF waves, various materials can be employed, each with its own benefits, limitations, and best-use scenarios. The most common materials used for RF shielding include metals, fabrics, and specialized coatings. Each material works in a different way to impede or absorb RF signals.

1. Metals

Metals are among the most effective materials for blocking RF waves due to their **high conductivity**. When RF waves encounter a metal surface, they are reflected, preventing them from passing through. Common metals used for RF shielding include:

- **Copper**: One of the most efficient materials for RF blocking due to its excellent conductivity. Copper is often used in industrial applications, such as Faraday cages and specialized shielding rooms.
- **Aluminum**: A lightweight and cost-effective alternative to copper, aluminum is commonly used in consumer-grade RF shielding products, including phone cases and foil-based shielding materials.
- **Steel**: While not as conductive as copper, steel is often used in larger-scale shielding applications, particularly in the construction of RF-blocking enclosures or buildings. Steel is also durable and can withstand environmental wear and tear.

2. Fabrics

RF-blocking fabrics are designed to absorb and dissipate the energy of RF waves, preventing them from passing through. These fabrics typically contain a combination of metallic fibers (such as silver, copper, or nickel) woven into textiles. The benefit of RF-blocking fabrics is that they are flexible, lightweight, and easy to integrate into various environments, from clothing to curtains to wall coverings.

- **Conductive Fabrics**: These fabrics are made from metal fibers and are designed to reflect or absorb RF signals. They can be used in items like **RF-blocking clothing**, **curtains**, and **blankets**.
- **Mesh Fabrics**: RF-blocking mesh is made with conductive threads in a grid pattern, allowing the material to be light and breathable while still providing effective shielding.

3. Coatings

RF-blocking coatings can be applied to various surfaces, such as windows, walls, and even vehicles. These coatings are typically made from conductive materials that create a barrier to RF waves. **Metalized coatings** are especially effective, as they form a thin layer of metal that reflects RF signals.

- **Conductive Paints**: These are special paints that contain metallic compounds and can be applied to walls, ceilings, and other surfaces to block RF waves. They are particularly useful in homes or offices where you want to shield a specific room or area.
- **Window Films**: Specialized films that can be applied to windows to block RF signals. These films are often used in office buildings or cars to reduce exposure to RF waves while still allowing for natural light to enter.

Benefits and Challenges of Blocking RF Waves

Blocking RF waves offers several significant benefits, but it also comes with its own set of challenges that must be carefully considered. Understanding both the advantages and limitations of RF shielding will help individuals make informed decisions when it comes to implementing these technologies.

Benefits of RF Blocking

1. **Health Protection**: By reducing exposure to RF waves, shielding can help mitigate the potential health risks associated with prolonged RF exposure, such as headaches, sleep disturbances, or long-term conditions like cancer (as noted in earlier chapters). Shielding is particularly important for vulnerable individuals, such as children and the elderly, who may be more susceptible to RF radiation.

2. **Increased Privacy and Security**: RF-blocking measures can protect sensitive communications from being intercepted. For example, Faraday cages or RF-blocking materials can prevent hacking attempts, such as man-in-the-middle attacks or unauthorized access to wireless networks.

3. **Reduced Interference**: RF waves can cause interference with other communication systems. In industries like aviation, military, or healthcare, reducing RF interference is crucial for ensuring the integrity and functionality of sensitive equipment. RF shielding helps ensure that devices operate without interference from other RF sources.

4. **Improved Productivity**: Reducing exposure to RF radiation can help minimize distractions and improve focus. For people who are sensitive to RF waves, working in RF-shielded environments can alleviate symptoms such as fatigue, brain fog, or anxiety.

Challenges of RF Blocking

1. **Cost**: High-quality RF-blocking materials, such as copper or specialized fabrics, can be expensive. Additionally, professional-grade shielding solutions, such as building a Faraday cage or installing RF-blocking windows, can involve significant costs that may not be affordable for everyone.

2. **Practicality**: Implementing RF shielding in everyday life can be challenging. For example, blocking signals at home or work can interfere with the convenience of using wireless devices like smartphones, laptops, or smart home technology. Finding a balance between convenience and protection is key when considering RF shielding solutions.

3. **Limited Coverage**: While RF-blocking materials are effective in specific areas, they may not provide 100% coverage. For instance, shielding a room with conductive paint or fabrics may block some signals but not others. Additionally, certain materials may degrade over time or lose their effectiveness.

4. **Unintended Consequences**: In some cases, blocking RF signals may interfere with the operation of essential devices. For example, blocking cellular signals may prevent the use of mobile phones, which could be problematic in emergencies. Similarly, excessive shielding could prevent devices like Wi-Fi routers or medical equipment from functioning correctly.

The Legality and Ethical Considerations of RF Shielding

As with any emerging technology, RF shielding comes with legal and ethical considerations that must be understood before implementing these solutions. Some of the key issues include:

1. Regulations and Compliance: In many countries, wireless communication systems are regulated by government agencies, such as the Federal Communications Commission (FCC) in the United States or the European Telecommunications Standards Institute (ETSI) in Europe. These agencies set rules for RF communication, including allowable power levels, frequency ranges, and interference prevention. While blocking RF signals for personal health or privacy reasons is generally allowed, blocking signals in a way that disrupts public or commercial systems (such as cell towers or broadcast signals) is illegal in many jurisdictions.

2. Ethical Use of RF Shielding: The ethical use of RF shielding involves considering the broader impact of blocking RF signals. For example, blocking RF signals in a shared public space or in a workplace could potentially disrupt communication or access to emergency services. It's important to ensure that RF-blocking practices do not inadvertently harm others or compromise essential services.

3. Personal vs Public Shielding: The question of whether individuals should be allowed to block RF signals that affect others is an ongoing debate. While it's reasonable to protect personal health or privacy, it becomes more complex when the shielding interferes with communal infrastructure, such as cellular networks or internet access.

Conclusion

RF blocking is a powerful tool for reducing exposure to RF waves and protecting health, privacy, and security. By understanding the materials and technologies used for RF shielding, as well as the benefits and challenges associated with these practices, individuals can make informed decisions about how to best protect themselves in an increasingly wireless world. Whether for personal well-being, privacy protection, or preventing interference, mastering RF shielding will play a crucial role in the future of communication and technology. However, it is important to consider the legal and ethical implications of these practices to ensure responsible and effective use of RF-blocking technologies.

Chapter 7: Shielding Materials and Technologies

In a world where wireless communication technologies are ubiquitous, understanding how to effectively shield yourself from harmful RF waves is essential. RF shielding materials are designed to block, absorb, or reflect electromagnetic waves, providing a barrier between the source of the RF signal and the area you want to protect. This chapter explores the various types of shielding materials and technologies, how they work, and practical applications of these solutions in everyday life.

Overview of Shielding Materials

Shielding materials come in various forms, from metals and conductive fabrics to specialized coatings and advanced technologies. Each material has unique properties that make it suited to specific RF-blocking applications. The effectiveness of these materials is determined by their ability to reflect, absorb, or dissipate the energy from RF waves.

1. Metals and Metallic Alloys

Metals are the most commonly used materials for RF shielding due to their ability to reflect and absorb RF waves efficiently. Their high electrical conductivity makes them ideal for blocking electromagnetic radiation, particularly at higher frequencies.

- **Copper**: Copper is one of the most effective metals for RF shielding because of its superior conductivity and ability to reflect RF waves. Copper is commonly used in **Faraday cages** and **shielding enclosures**, where it forms a barrier that blocks external RF signals. It is widely used in industrial applications, including in military and aerospace technologies.
- **Aluminum**: Aluminum is a more affordable alternative to copper, though it is less conductive. It is commonly used for shielding purposes in **consumer products** like **RF-blocking bags**, **cellphone cases**, and **windows**. Aluminum's lightweight properties make it a preferred choice for large-scale applications, such as shielding buildings and electronic enclosures.
- **Steel**: Steel, especially **stainless steel**, is another metal that can be used for RF shielding. While it is not as conductive as copper or aluminum, it still offers significant attenuation of RF signals. Steel is particularly useful in industrial and commercial applications due to its durability and resistance to environmental wear.

2. Conductive Fabrics

Conductive fabrics are textiles embedded with metallic fibers, allowing them to block RF waves while remaining flexible and lightweight. These materials are ideal for use in portable and consumer-grade products that need to offer some level of shielding without the weight or rigidity of metal sheets.

- **Nickel-Copper and Silver-Coated Fabrics**: These fabrics typically feature a blend of **nickel-copper** or **silver-coated** fibers woven into the textile. They are used in products such as **RF-blocking clothing** (e.g., shirts, hats, and pants), **curtains**, **bed canopies**, and **blankets**. Conductive fabrics can shield from a range of RF frequencies, depending on their construction.
- **Carbon Fiber and Polyester Blends**: Some fabrics combine conductive fibers with non-metallic materials, offering RF shielding alongside durability and comfort. These fabrics are commonly found in **smartphone cases**, **laptop sleeves**, and **RF-blocking bags** that help protect electronic devices from external signals.

3. Specialized Coatings

Another effective method of shielding RF signals is through the application of conductive coatings. These coatings can be applied to walls, windows, furniture, or even electronics to create an RF-blocking barrier.

- **Metalized Coatings**: Metalized coatings are thin layers of metal (usually aluminum) that are applied to surfaces, like glass or plastic. These coatings are often used in **window films** or **protective screens** for electronics to block RF waves without significantly altering the appearance of the material.
- **Conductive Paints**: Conductive paints are specially formulated with metallic compounds, such as **copper**, **silver**, or **nickel**, to allow them to block RF signals. These paints can be applied to walls, ceilings, or furniture to create RF-shielded environments. Conductive paints are especially useful for small, enclosed spaces or specific areas within a home or office.

4. Metamaterials

Metamaterials are artificially engineered materials designed to have specific properties not found in naturally occurring substances. These materials can be used to manipulate and control electromagnetic waves, including RF signals, in innovative ways.

- **Electromagnetic Band Gap (EBG) Materials**: EBG materials are engineered to block RF waves at certain frequencies, providing a highly specialized form of shielding. These materials are used in advanced **military**, **aerospace**, and **telecommunications** applications, where precise control over electromagnetic interference (EMI) is required.
- **Photonic Crystals**: Photonic crystals are similar to EBG materials but are designed to control electromagnetic waves across a broader range of frequencies. These materials are still in the experimental phase but hold promise for future RF shielding applications in highly sensitive environments.

How RF Shielding Works

RF shielding works by either **reflecting** or **absorbing** the electromagnetic waves. The effectiveness of a material depends on several factors, including its conductivity, thickness, and the frequency of the RF waves it is intended to block. Let's explore how each method of shielding operates.

1. Reflection

Reflection occurs when RF waves strike a conductive surface, such as metal, and are bounced back, preventing them from passing through the material. Materials that are highly reflective, like copper and aluminum, are excellent at blocking RF waves. The metal surface prevents the waves from entering a protected space, such as a Faraday cage or shielded room.

2. Absorption

Absorption occurs when RF waves are absorbed by a material and converted into another form of energy, such as heat. Conductive fabrics and specialized coatings, like metalized paints, often rely on absorption to dissipate RF energy. While these materials are typically not as effective as metals at **reflecting** RF waves, they still offer substantial protection by reducing the intensity of incoming signals.

3. Penetration Loss

Penetration loss refers to the reduction in signal strength as RF waves pass through a shielding material. The effectiveness of a shielding material in reducing signal strength is determined by the material's **attenuation rate**. A material with high attenuation reduces the signal strength more effectively, making it harder for RF waves to pass through.

The effectiveness of shielding materials can vary depending on the frequency of the RF signal. For instance, **low-frequency signals** (such as those used in AM radio) may be easier to block, while **high-frequency signals** (such as those used in 5G networks) may require more advanced shielding materials.

Practical Applications of Shielding Technology

RF shielding technology is used in various practical applications across industries and in everyday life. Below are some examples of how shielding materials and technologies are applied to reduce exposure to RF waves:

1. Faraday Cages

A Faraday cage is a conductive enclosure that blocks external RF signals from entering a protected space. Faraday cages can be made from metal mesh or sheets and are used in environments where high levels of shielding are required, such as in **laboratories, military installations**, or **data centers**. A typical Faraday cage may be used to shield sensitive electronics or data from RF interference or unauthorized access.

2. Consumer Products

Many consumer products now include RF shielding to protect individuals from RF exposure. These products include:

- **RF-blocking phone cases**: Designed to block incoming and outgoing signals from smartphones, preventing radiation from reaching the body.
- **Laptop shields**: Special bags or covers designed to shield electronic devices from external RF signals, protecting data from hacking attempts.
- **Anti-RFID tags**: Used in **credit cards** and **passports**, these tags shield sensitive information from being scanned by RFID readers.

3. Home and Office Shielding

In homes and offices, RF shielding can be used to create spaces with minimal RF exposure. This includes:

- **RF-blocking window films**: These films prevent RF waves from entering or exiting a building, providing privacy and reducing exposure to external RF sources.
- **Shielded rooms**: For those concerned with RF exposure, entire rooms or offices can be shielded using conductive fabrics, paints, or metal mesh to create a low-RF environment.
- **EMF protection devices**: Small devices that reduce EMF levels in specific areas, such as **bedrooms** or **workspaces**, to minimize exposure to RF radiation during sleep or work.

4. Transportation

RF shielding is also important in transportation. For instance, **automobiles** are increasingly equipped with RF-blocking materials to prevent interference with GPS systems, mobile phones, and other RF-based technologies. In **aviation**, RF shielding is used to protect sensitive communication systems and to prevent unwanted RF interference.

Conclusion

RF shielding is a vital tool for reducing exposure to harmful electromagnetic radiation, protecting privacy, and preventing interference in both personal and professional environments. The materials and technologies discussed in this chapter—metals, fabrics, coatings, and advanced metamaterials—each offer unique properties and benefits depending on the specific shielding requirements. By understanding the various options and how they work, individuals and organizations can make informed decisions about how to effectively shield themselves from unwanted RF exposure, creating safer and more secure environments for both work and leisure.

Chapter 8: DIY RF Blocking Methods

For many individuals seeking to reduce exposure to Radio Frequency (RF) waves, creating DIY RF-blocking solutions can be an affordable and effective approach. While professional-grade shielding materials and technologies offer high performance, they can be expensive and may not be necessary for everyone. This chapter explores how you can create your own RF-blocking solutions using household items, simple materials, and basic tools. We will also look at how to build a **basic Faraday cage**—one of the most common and effective ways to block RF signals—and examine the effectiveness and limitations of DIY methods.

How to Create DIY RF-Blocking Solutions at Home

DIY RF-blocking methods are widely accessible and can be achieved with materials that are relatively easy to obtain. Whether you're trying to shield a specific room, reduce exposure to certain devices, or protect sensitive electronics, here are some approaches you can take:

1. Using Household Items to Block RF Signals

Many household items can help create a makeshift shield from RF waves. By leveraging the conductive or absorbent properties of common materials, you can block or reduce the strength of RF signals. The key is to choose materials that have the ability to reflect or absorb the energy from RF waves. Here are some examples:

- **Aluminum Foil**: One of the easiest and most cost-effective DIY shielding materials is aluminum foil. It is highly conductive, lightweight, and can reflect RF waves effectively. To create an RF shield using aluminum foil, simply cover a device (such as a smartphone or router) or a surface (like a window or door) with multiple layers of foil. For example, wrapping a phone in several layers of aluminum foil will block most RF signals, making it harder for the phone to send or receive data.
- **Metal Mesh**: Mesh made from metal, such as **copper** or **aluminum**, can be an effective barrier to RF signals. You can use wire mesh to cover windows or doors in areas where you want to block RF waves. These materials will not only reflect the waves but also absorb some of the RF energy.
- **Fabric with Metallic Fibers**: Some fabrics, such as **window curtains** or **blankets** embedded with metallic threads, can help block RF signals. These fabrics are typically available in **RF-blocking** stores, but you can also make your own using conductive thread or by adding layers of metallic foil into the fabric.
- **Cardboard or Wood**: While not as effective as metals or conductive fabrics, thicker materials like **cardboard** or **wood** can provide some attenuation of RF signals, particularly at lower frequencies. These can be used in combination with other shielding materials to enhance effectiveness.

2. **Creating a Faraday Cage**

A **Faraday cage** is one of the most well-known and effective methods of blocking RF signals. It works by surrounding a space or device with a conductive material that shields the inside from external RF fields. The conductive material reflects or absorbs RF waves, preventing them from reaching the items inside the cage.

To build a basic Faraday cage at home, follow these steps:

Materials Needed:

- Conductive material (such as **aluminum foil, copper mesh,** or **conductive fabric**)
- A box or container (such as a **metal trash can, cardboard box,** or **plastic box**)
- Tape or glue to secure the material

Step-by-Step Guide:

1. **Choose the Container**: Find a container that can fully encase the device you want to shield. A metal trash can or a plastic box lined with metal is often the best choice. Ensure the container is large enough to fit the device without obstruction.
2. **Prepare the Shielding Material**: Cut the conductive material (e.g., aluminum foil or copper mesh) to the required size to line the inside of the container. If you're using **aluminum foil**, you'll need multiple layers to ensure a stronger barrier.
3. **Line the Container**: Cover the entire inside of the container with your shielding material, ensuring that there are no gaps or exposed areas. For the Faraday cage to work properly, the conductive material must fully surround the device.
4. **Seal the Gaps**: To enhance the shielding, make sure to seal any gaps where RF signals could penetrate. This might include seams along the edges of the container or areas where the material doesn't fully overlap. Use **electrical tape** or **conductive adhesive** to secure the shielding material and eliminate potential leaks.
5. **Test the Cage**: Place a mobile phone or other wireless device inside the Faraday cage, close the lid, and try calling the phone or sending a text message. If the phone is unable to receive the signal, the cage is working as intended. For optimal performance, the material should fully block any RF signals from reaching the device.

A Faraday cage can be used to block signals from **cell phones**, **Wi-Fi routers**, **radio signals**, and other RF-emitting devices. Larger Faraday cages can be built for shielding entire rooms, while smaller, more portable cages can be used to protect sensitive equipment or electronics from RF interference or hacking.

Effectiveness and Limitations of DIY Methods

DIY RF-blocking solutions are an accessible way to protect yourself from unwanted RF exposure. However, there are limitations to the effectiveness of these methods that must be understood.

1. Effectiveness of Materials

- **Aluminum Foil**: While aluminum foil is an excellent and affordable material for RF shielding, it has limitations. It may block most RF signals, but its effectiveness diminishes with thinner layers or if the foil has holes or gaps. Foil wrapped around a device might not block all RF frequencies, especially higher frequencies used in **5G** or **Wi-Fi** networks.
- **Metals and Mesh**: Copper and aluminum mesh are more effective than foil, particularly at higher frequencies. However, when using mesh materials, the spacing between the wires or the holes in the mesh can allow RF signals to pass through, especially for higher-frequency signals. For better results, choose a **fine mesh** or multiple layers.
- **Fabrics**: Conductive fabrics offer flexibility and comfort, but they may not be as efficient as metals. The level of shielding depends on the fabric's **metallic fiber content** and the **frequency range** it is designed to block. The best fabrics are those designed specifically for RF blocking, as they are woven with higher concentrations of metallic fibers.

2. Practical Limitations

- **Partial Coverage**: DIY shielding often results in partial coverage, which may leave some areas exposed to RF signals. For example, a Faraday cage made of foil may shield a device but could still leave small gaps along seams, where RF waves might penetrate.

- **Limited Frequency Blocking**: DIY materials may not effectively block all RF frequencies, especially those in the higher ranges (such as **5G** or **Wi-Fi 6** frequencies). Professional-grade shielding materials are more targeted and efficient at blocking specific frequency bands.

- **Inconvenience**: DIY RF-blocking methods are effective in specific circumstances, but they can be inconvenient for daily use. For instance, wrapping a phone in aluminum foil for shielding can make it difficult to use. Additionally, while Faraday cages are excellent for protecting electronics, they can be bulky and impractical for frequent access.

Conclusion

Creating DIY RF-blocking solutions at home is an effective, cost-efficient way to reduce exposure to unwanted RF signals and protect your privacy and health. Simple materials like aluminum foil, metal mesh, and conductive fabrics can provide varying levels of protection against RF radiation. Building a Faraday cage is one of the most effective methods for creating a fully enclosed shield for electronic devices or sensitive equipment. However, it's important to recognize the limitations of DIY methods, such as partial coverage, limited frequency blocking, and practical challenges. Despite these limitations, DIY RF shielding can serve as a first step for individuals looking to mitigate their exposure to RF waves without the need for expensive professional-grade solutions.

Chapter 9: Advanced RF Shielding Solutions

As awareness of the potential risks associated with Radio Frequency (RF) exposure continues to grow, many individuals and organizations are seeking professional-grade RF shielding solutions to effectively mitigate their exposure. While DIY methods can provide some level of protection, advanced RF shielding technologies offer much higher levels of effectiveness. This chapter explores the professional-grade RF shielding options available, how to customize RF shielding for different environments—such as the home, office, or vehicle—and examines the technologies used in military, corporate, and industrial sectors to block RF waves. Additionally, we'll explore case studies of advanced shielding solutions to highlight how these methods have been implemented successfully.

Professional-Grade RF Shielding Options

Advanced RF shielding solutions are designed to provide comprehensive protection against high levels of RF radiation, often used in sensitive environments where minimizing RF interference or exposure is critical. These solutions are typically made from materials and technologies that are not only highly effective but also durable enough for long-term use.

1. Faraday Cages and Faraday Rooms

A **Faraday cage** is a fully enclosed, conductive material structure that blocks external electric fields, including RF signals. Faraday cages are one of the most effective and secure methods of shielding from RF waves and are commonly used in environments that require high levels of protection, such as government buildings, military facilities, and scientific laboratories.

- **Faraday Rooms**: A Faraday cage can be a single item or a room in which all the walls, windows, and doors are lined with a conductive material. These rooms are designed to block all incoming and outgoing RF signals, making them ideal for use in secure locations. Faraday rooms are often found in locations that handle sensitive data or require RF isolation to prevent interference with critical systems.
- **Custom Faraday Cages**: For individuals or businesses that require personalized RF shielding, custom Faraday cages can be built. These can vary from small enclosures for personal electronics to larger, room-sized structures for offices or research labs. The shielding material used in a Faraday cage—such as **copper mesh** or **aluminum foil**—must be carefully chosen based on the required frequency range and effectiveness.

2. Shielded Rooms and Enclosures

For larger applications, RF shielding can be built into the very infrastructure of a room or building. Shielded rooms and enclosures are created by incorporating specialized materials that block RF waves while also maintaining usability and aesthetic appeal.

- **Modular Shielded Rooms**: These rooms are constructed using prefabricated panels made of metal and other conductive materials. These panels are designed to prevent RF waves from penetrating the walls, ceiling, and floor, making them ideal for businesses and laboratories that need to isolate RF-sensitive equipment or personnel.
- **Metalized Paint and Coatings**: In some cases, applying a conductive coating or metalized paint to walls, ceilings, and floors can provide an additional layer of shielding. These coatings are typically made from materials such as **nickel**, **copper**, or **aluminum** and can be applied to the interior of walls or to surfaces that require RF isolation.

3. Advanced Window Films

Windows are one of the most significant points of RF entry into a building, and protecting them with advanced shielding technologies is essential. **Metalized window films** are designed to block RF waves while allowing light to pass through. These films are made from thin layers of metal that reflect or absorb RF signals, providing protection without the need for heavy metal window coverings.

Smart Glass

smart glass

Customizing RF Shielding for Different Environments

The choice of RF shielding material and solution will depend on the specific environment you are trying to protect. Customizing shielding to the needs of a particular location is essential to achieving the desired level of protection. Here, we look at different environments—home, office, and vehicles—and explore the specific shielding needs for each.

1. Home RF Shielding

In a home setting, RF shielding is often used to reduce exposure to mobile phones, Wi-Fi routers, baby monitors, and other RF-emitting devices. For those concerned with health or privacy, here are some effective strategies:

- **Shielding Specific Rooms**: You can create an RF-free zone within your home by shielding specific rooms, such as bedrooms or home offices. Using **conductive fabrics, RF-blocking window films**, or **Faraday enclosures** for electronics can provide significant protection without the need to shield the entire house.
- **Shielding Wireless Devices**: For devices like routers or smart home technology, using **RF-blocking covers, Faraday pouches**, or strategically positioning them away from areas where you spend most of your time can help reduce exposure.

2. Office RF Shielding

In office environments, RF shielding can help reduce interference from wireless devices and improve the security of communications. Here are some options for workplace protection:

- **RF Shielded Workstations**: For workplaces dealing with sensitive information, **RF shielded desks** or **workstations** can provide protection against RF interference. These workstations often include shielding on the walls and desk surfaces, as well as enclosures for sensitive devices.
- **Building-Wide Shielding**: Larger offices or companies dealing with classified information may require **whole-building RF shielding**. This can include applying metalized coatings on walls, installing **RF-blocking window films**, or building custom RF-proof rooms within the office to isolate sensitive activities.

3. Vehicle RF Shielding

RF signals can interfere with the proper functioning of automotive systems and also expose individuals to unwanted radiation. Shielding your vehicle from RF waves is essential for those concerned with both security and health.

- **RF-Blocking Window Films**: Many vehicles now use **RF-blocking window films** to prevent signals from entering or exiting the vehicle. These films are particularly effective at blocking signals from external sources like **cell towers**, **GPS satellites**, and **Wi-Fi** networks.
- **Custom RF-Blocking Enclosures**: For high-security vehicles or military-grade applications, custom RF-blocking enclosures can be built into the vehicle's structure. This often includes metallic coatings and mesh materials in key areas such as the doors, roof, and engine compartment.

Technologies Used in Military and Corporate Sectors for RF Blocking

RF shielding is critical in both the military and corporate sectors, where the security of communications, data, and equipment is paramount. The technologies used in these sectors often go beyond simple shielding solutions and incorporate advanced techniques for preventing RF interference, interception, and hacking.

1. Military-Grade Shielding

Military applications require the highest levels of RF shielding due to the need for secure communications, data protection, and electronic warfare capabilities. Some of the technologies employed include:

- **Electronic Warfare (EW) Systems**: These systems are designed to block or disrupt enemy communications and radar systems using advanced RF jamming and spoofing techniques. EW systems rely heavily on sophisticated shielding and the ability to transmit interference at specific frequencies.
- **Hardened Enclosures**: Military installations often use **hardened enclosures**—customized Faraday cages and rooms equipped with advanced shielding materials—to protect sensitive equipment from RF interference or unauthorized surveillance.

2. Corporate and Data Center Shielding

In the corporate sector, especially in data centers and financial institutions, RF shielding is crucial to protect against hacking, data breaches, and the interception of sensitive communications. Technologies used in corporate environments include:

- **Secure Communication Systems**: Companies that deal with high-value data use **secure communication lines** that include RF-blocking and jamming technologies to prevent data interception. These systems may also employ encrypted communication protocols to add an additional layer of security.
- **Data Center Shielding**: Data centers rely on **RF shielding rooms** and **enclosures** to protect critical data servers and sensitive information from external RF threats. This often involves using **metalized mesh** and **conductive materials** that block RF signals from infiltrating server rooms.

Case Studies of Advanced Shielding Solutions

1. A Military Research Facility

A leading military research facility implemented a Faraday cage solution to protect its research on electronic warfare. The facility was designed to completely block RF signals from external sources, ensuring that sensitive communication equipment could not be intercepted. The building was lined with **copper mesh** and equipped with RF-blocking doors and windows, preventing any RF signals from entering or exiting the premises.

2. Corporate Office in a High-Risk Location

A financial institution located in a high-risk area for espionage used RF-blocking technologies to protect their communication systems. The company installed **shielded workstations** and **RF-blocking window films** to safeguard their operations. Additionally, they implemented **metalized coatings** on walls to further isolate sensitive departments and minimize the risk of external RF interference.

Conclusion

Advanced RF shielding solutions are an essential part of protecting sensitive information, ensuring secure communications, and safeguarding health. From Faraday cages and shielded rooms to custom RF-blocking materials and coatings, these technologies provide robust protection in high-risk environments such as military facilities, corporate offices, and personal spaces. By understanding the various shielding options and customizing them for specific needs, individuals and organizations can significantly reduce their exposure to harmful RF waves and create more secure, RF-controlled environments.

Chapter 10: Shielding in Everyday Life

In our increasingly connected world, where wireless technologies permeate nearly every aspect of our daily lives, managing RF exposure has become an essential aspect of maintaining personal health, security, and privacy. While many individuals are familiar with basic RF shielding techniques for specific devices or environments, the challenge lies in implementing shielding practices in everyday life—at home, at work, and even in public spaces. This chapter explores how to incorporate effective RF shielding strategies into your routine and the importance of balancing protection with convenience.

How to Implement RF Shielding in Your Personal Life

Implementing RF shielding in your personal life can seem daunting at first, but by understanding the basics and strategically applying shielding solutions, it becomes much more manageable. Below are the key areas in your life where shielding can make a significant difference.

1. Blocking Signals at Home

Your home is where you spend the most time, making it a crucial area to focus on when it comes to reducing RF exposure. The good news is that there are several simple steps you can take to shield your living space.

- **Wi-Fi and Routers**: Wi-Fi routers are a primary source of RF radiation in most homes. While it's impractical to completely eliminate Wi-Fi, you can reduce exposure by strategically positioning your router. Place it in a less frequently used area of the house, such as a hallway or utility room, and ensure it is not close to where you sleep or spend extended periods of time. Turning off the Wi-Fi at night is also a simple step to minimize exposure during sleep.
- **Smartphones and Tablets**: Phones, tablets, and other wireless devices are common sources of RF waves. **RF-blocking cases** and **Faraday pouches** are great for protecting your devices when not in use. For smartphones, consider **airplane mode** when you don't need the device to transmit, or place your phone in a **Faraday cage** to block incoming and outgoing signals.
- **Baby Monitors**: Many modern baby monitors operate on RF signals, making them potential sources of exposure in your child's room. Look for **low-emission baby monitors**, or consider using **video monitors** that don't rely on RF technology, such as those that operate through wired systems or **digital systems** with lower radiation output.

- **Microwave Ovens**: Microwave ovens emit **microwave radiation**, which is a form of RF. If you are concerned about exposure, it is a good idea to avoid standing directly in front of the microwave when it is in use. You can also shield the space by keeping the microwave in a separate room, or by purchasing an **RF-blocking microwave cover** or **RF-shielding curtains** for kitchen windows.

2. Shielding at Work

Many individuals spend a significant amount of their day in office environments, where the concentration of RF-emitting devices—such as cell phones, laptops, and Wi-Fi networks—can be high. Here are several strategies to protect yourself in a workplace setting.

- **Workstation Shielding**: Set up your workstation with the intent to shield yourself from RF exposure. Use **RF-blocking desk mats** or place **RF-blocking fabrics** on your desk. Additionally, **shielding phone cases** for your office phone and **wired headphones** instead of Bluetooth headsets can significantly reduce your exposure during long hours of communication.
- **Wi-Fi Router Placement**: Similar to your home, consider moving the office Wi-Fi router or access points to areas away from where you work. Placing routers in storage closets or less-frequented spaces can help minimize your exposure.
- **Use of Ethernet Cables**: Opt for wired internet connections rather than relying on Wi-Fi, especially if you are working in a **high-RF environment**. Using **Ethernet cables** for both workstations and printers not only reduces your exposure to Wi-Fi signals but can also increase the stability and speed of your internet connection.
- **Laptop Shielding**: If you need to work with a laptop or portable device, make use of **laptop shielding mats** that can absorb or reflect RF radiation. You can also minimize exposure by placing the device on a **non-metallic surface** such as a wooden or stone desk, rather than a metal one, as metals can exacerbate the signal exposure.

3. Shielding in Public Spaces

Even in public spaces, RF shielding can play an important role in reducing unnecessary exposure. Whether traveling on public transportation, visiting cafes, or attending events, here are ways to shield yourself from RF waves:

- **Portable RF Protection**: Use **RF-blocking bags** to shield your electronics, especially when traveling. These bags can help block any incoming RF signals that might be used for tracking or tampering with your devices. Similarly, **RF-blocking wallets** and **passport holders** are useful for protecting your personal information from RF-based hacking.

- **Public Wi-Fi**: Public Wi-Fi networks can expose you to not only RF radiation but also security risks. Avoid connecting to unsecured or public networks without using a **VPN** (Virtual Private Network) to encrypt your data. Additionally, **turn off Wi-Fi** and **Bluetooth** on your devices when not in use, as they continuously emit RF signals even when you're not actively connected.

- **Shielding Headphones**: Bluetooth headphones emit RF signals, which can be a concern for some people, particularly when used for extended periods. Look for **wired headphones** or **shielding Bluetooth devices** that reduce RF exposure while still offering the functionality you need.

- **Public Transport and Waiting Areas**: On public transportation, where RF signals from cell towers and mobile devices can overlap, keep your device in **airplane mode** or use an **RF-blocking pouch** to minimize exposure. If you're in a waiting area with many people on their phones, consider sitting further away from high-traffic areas.

The Balance Between Convenience and Protection

While it is possible to implement RF shielding throughout your life, it's important to recognize that there are trade-offs between **convenience** and **protection**. Shielding yourself from RF signals can improve your health and privacy, but it can also impact the functionality of certain devices and services.

- **Accessibility vs. Protection**: For example, placing your phone in a Faraday pouch can block RF signals, but it will also prevent you from receiving calls, messages, or notifications. Similarly, turning off Wi-Fi or using wired internet connections can reduce exposure, but it may limit your ability to access high-speed wireless networks. Consider your needs and prioritize shielding in areas that matter most to your health or security.
- **Work-Life Balance**: In a professional environment, shielding devices may impact the convenience of remote working or communicating through wireless methods. It's important to strike a balance between using shielding technologies that protect your privacy and health while still allowing you to perform your job efficiently.
- **Adaptation**: Over time, you may find that your initial adjustments to shield from RF waves become second nature. As you continue to integrate these habits into your life, you may adapt to the more secure, yet less intrusive, methods of managing RF exposure.

Conclusion

Shielding from RF waves in everyday life is not about disconnecting entirely from technology; rather, it's about finding a healthy balance. By strategically implementing shielding measures at home, at work, and in public spaces, you can significantly reduce your exposure to potentially harmful RF radiation while maintaining the convenience and connectivity that modern life requires. Whether it's using RF-blocking materials for specific devices, opting for wired connections, or utilizing portable shielding options, taking proactive steps to manage RF exposure allows you to take control of your health, privacy, and security in an increasingly RF-powered world.

Chapter 11: RF Blocking in the Home

Our homes are meant to be safe havens, places where we can relax, recharge, and spend quality time with our loved ones. However, with the increasing prevalence of wireless devices—such as smartphones, laptops, Wi-Fi routers, smart home systems, and baby monitors—our homes have become sources of constant exposure to Radio Frequency (RF) radiation. For those concerned with the potential health and privacy risks of RF waves, it becomes crucial to implement effective shielding strategies within the home.

This chapter explores various methods to block RF signals in your living space, including RF-blocking materials for walls, windows, and furniture. We will also discuss how to manage the RF interference from specific devices like cellphones, routers, and baby monitors, as well as how to protect your home from smart home RF interference.

Shielding Your Living Space

Creating an RF-free environment in your home can feel like a complex task due to the pervasive nature of RF signals. However, with the right materials and planning, you can significantly reduce the exposure from household devices. Below are some areas to focus on to block RF signals effectively.

1. Blocking RF Signals from the Outside

Your home is exposed to RF signals from the outside world, such as those coming from cell towers, radio stations, and even nearby Wi-Fi networks. These signals can seep through windows, walls, and other materials. One way to block these external signals is by using **RF-blocking materials** that are specifically designed for construction or retrofitting purposes.

- **Metalized Window Films**: These films are designed to block RF signals from entering through windows while still allowing light to pass through. They are made from thin layers of metal, such as **aluminum** or **silver**, that reflect or absorb RF energy. Applying metalized window films to your windows can significantly reduce RF exposure, especially in urban or high-traffic areas where signal interference from cell towers or broadcast stations is common.
- **RF-blocking Paints**: Special **conductive paints** are available that can be applied to walls, ceilings, and floors to block RF signals from entering your home. These paints contain **metallic compounds**, such as **copper** or **nickel**, that reflect RF waves. This is especially useful for people living in areas with heavy signal traffic or those wanting to create a shielded room within their home.
- **Shielding Curtains**: Another option is **RF-blocking curtains** made from conductive fabrics or metalized materials. These curtains can be hung over windows to block RF signals while maintaining the aesthetic of your home. They are especially useful in rooms where you spend a lot of time, such as bedrooms or home offices.

2. Shielding Walls and Furniture

Your home's walls and furniture can be reinforced to block RF signals effectively. Here are a few ways to shield these elements:

- **Conductive Wallpaper**: There are special wallpapers available that incorporate metal fibers or conductive materials. When applied to your walls, these wallpapers provide an additional layer of RF shielding that can help protect your living space from RF radiation coming from external sources or nearby wireless devices.
- **RF-blocking Fabrics**: For areas that are particularly susceptible to RF exposure, such as near routers or electrical equipment, you can cover furniture or create custom enclosures using **RF-blocking fabrics**. These fabrics are often made from metalized threads and can be used to cover **couches**, **chairs**, **bed frames**, and **bookshelves**, particularly in areas where you spend a lot of time.
- **Shielded Furniture**: Some furniture items, such as **desks**, **bookshelves**, and **storage units**, can be custom-built or purchased with built-in RF shielding. These can be useful for containing RF-emitting devices or creating a barrier between you and the sources of RF radiation.

Blocking Specific Devices

Certain devices in your home, such as cellphones, Wi-Fi routers, and baby monitors, are significant sources of RF radiation. By shielding or managing these devices, you can reduce the level of exposure in your home.

1. Cellphones and Tablets

Cellphones and tablets emit RF waves during communication, especially when they are actively sending or receiving data. To minimize exposure, consider the following approaches:

- **Use Airplane Mode**: When you're not using your phone for calls or data, activate **airplane mode** to stop it from emitting RF waves. This is especially important when you're sleeping or spending time in a small, enclosed space.
- **RF-blocking Phone Cases**: There are several **RF-blocking phone cases** available on the market that reduce the exposure to RF signals while still allowing your device to function. These cases are often lined with materials like **copper**, **silver**, or **aluminum** that block the RF waves from reaching your body.
- **Avoid Carrying Phones Close to Your Body**: Try to avoid keeping your phone in your pocket or on your body for extended periods of time. Instead, keep it in a bag, purse, or RF-blocking pouch, especially when it is not in use.

2. Wi-Fi Routers

Wi-Fi routers are one of the primary sources of RF radiation in many homes, transmitting RF signals continuously. To reduce exposure, consider the following:

- **Turn Off Wi-Fi When Not in Use**: If you don't need Wi-Fi for extended periods, turning it off can reduce RF exposure significantly. Consider turning off your router at night or during times when you don't need internet access.
- **Relocate the Router**: Place your Wi-Fi router in a less frequently used area, such as a hallway or closet, away from where you sleep or spend a lot of time. Ensure that it is not positioned directly next to seating areas or beds to minimize direct exposure.
- **Use Wired Connections**: If possible, opt for a **wired Ethernet connection** rather than relying on Wi-Fi. Wired connections eliminate the need for wireless signals and can improve your internet speed and security at the same time.

3. Baby Monitors

Modern **baby monitors** can be a significant source of RF exposure, as they transmit wireless signals to monitor and communicate with your child. To protect against this exposure:

- **Opt for Wired Monitors**: Consider using **wired baby monitors** that don't emit RF signals. These models use cables to transmit audio or video feeds to the parent unit, eliminating the need for wireless communication.
- **Minimize Proximity**: If you use a wireless baby monitor, try to place the transmitter as far away from your child as possible while still ensuring that it works effectively.

Smart Home RF Interference and How to Manage It

With the rise of smart homes, many devices are constantly emitting RF signals—such as **smart thermostats, smart speakers, motion sensors**, and **smart lights**. While these devices offer convenience, they also contribute to your overall RF exposure. Here's how to manage smart home RF interference:

- **Limit Unnecessary Smart Devices**: Be mindful of the number of smart devices you use in your home. Each additional device adds more RF radiation to the environment, so it's important to choose the ones that provide the most value and reduce the number of unnecessary devices.
- **Use Zoning and Scheduling**: For devices that you cannot eliminate, consider using scheduling features to limit when they are active. For example, you can set smart thermostats to operate only during certain hours or use **smart plugs** to turn off devices when they are not needed.
- **Faraday Enclosures for Devices**: If you have particularly sensitive devices or areas in your home, you can use **Faraday pouches** or **enclosures** to block RF signals. These can be used for everything from smart meters to control panels for smart home systems.

Conclusion

Creating an RF-safe home doesn't require eliminating technology entirely—it's about striking a balance. By using RF-blocking materials for walls, windows, and furniture, shielding specific devices like phones and Wi-Fi routers, and managing the interference from smart home devices, you can significantly reduce your exposure to RF waves. The steps you take will depend on your level of concern and the importance of RF-free zones in your home. Whether it's improving the quality of your sleep, enhancing privacy, or ensuring better health, shielding your home from RF radiation is an essential component of mastering the art of disconnecting in our RF-powered world.

Chapter 12: RF Protection in the Workplace

In modern workplaces, RF (Radio Frequency) radiation is an unavoidable part of the technological landscape. From Wi-Fi networks and Bluetooth devices to cellphones and wireless communication systems, RF signals are essential for the day-to-day operation of businesses and offices. However, with the growing awareness of the potential health effects of prolonged RF exposure, it has become increasingly important to take proactive steps to reduce this exposure, particularly in environments where employees are regularly working with wireless technology. This chapter discusses the risks of RF exposure in office environments, methods to reduce RF exposure at work, how to implement RF-blocking technology in workspaces, and the legal obligations and workplace safety standards that employers and employees should be aware of.

Risks of RF Exposure in Office Environments

Office environments are filled with various devices that emit RF radiation. While the signals may be low in intensity, prolonged exposure can accumulate over time, potentially leading to health risks. Some of the common sources of RF exposure in the workplace include:

1. Wi-Fi Networks

Wi-Fi routers are often one of the most significant sources of RF radiation in offices, constantly emitting signals to allow wireless connectivity. Depending on the proximity of employees to the router, exposure can vary. Those who work in close proximity to the router may experience higher levels of exposure, particularly if the router is located in an open area.

2. Cellphones and Smartphones

Smartphones and office phones, whether on or off, emit RF waves when searching for signals, especially when there is poor reception. Employees who keep their phones on their desks or in their pockets are exposed to ongoing RF emissions.

3. Bluetooth Devices

Bluetooth technology is widely used for communication between devices such as headsets, keyboards, and speakers. These devices, like Wi-Fi, emit RF radiation continuously when in use, adding to the overall RF exposure in an office environment.

4. Cordless Phones

While cordless phones may seem like a thing of the past with the advent of smartphones, they are still commonly used in many office spaces. These phones operate using RF signals, and depending on the model, their base stations can emit substantial radiation.

5. Wireless Printers and Other Devices

Many office devices, including printers, scanners, and other equipment, are now wireless, contributing to the RF environment of the workspace. These devices can often emit signals when in use, and employees may not be aware of their contribution to the overall RF exposure.

Methods to Reduce RF Exposure at Work

Given the presence of RF-emitting devices in modern offices, reducing exposure requires a multifaceted approach. Here are some practical steps that can be taken:

1. Positioning of Wireless Routers

One of the easiest ways to reduce exposure is by strategically placing Wi-Fi routers. **Router placement** is crucial: avoid placing routers in open areas where employees spend extended periods, such as near desks, workstations, or meeting rooms. Instead, consider placing them in less frequented areas, such as corridors or utility rooms, to limit direct exposure.

2. Use of Wired Connections

Where possible, opt for **wired Ethernet connections** instead of relying on Wi-Fi. Wired connections eliminate the need for constant RF signal transmission and can improve internet speed and stability. For employees who primarily use laptops or desktops, encourage the use of Ethernet cables to connect to the internet and printers.

3. Minimizing Bluetooth Use

While Bluetooth is useful for connectivity, it does contribute to RF exposure. Encourage employees to use **wired headphones** and **keyboards** instead of Bluetooth models. Additionally, turn off Bluetooth functionality on devices when it is not in use.

4. Cellphone Management

Encourage employees to **turn off their cellphones** when not in use, particularly during meetings or overnight. Consider implementing policies for **airplane mode** during working hours, where phones are placed away from desks to limit exposure. Providing **RF-blocking pouches** or **Faraday bags** for employees to store their phones during work hours can also reduce exposure.

5. Limit the Use of Wireless Office Equipment

Evaluate the necessity of using **wireless office equipment**. For example, switch to **wired phones** or **USB printers** when possible. If a wireless printer is required, place it in an area away from employee workstations. Additionally, consider the possibility of turning off wireless devices during non-working hours to further reduce exposure.

6. RF Shielding Materials

If there is a need to create RF-free zones within the office, **RF-blocking materials** such as **conductive paints**, **Faraday cages**, and **shielded enclosures** can be used. These materials can be applied to office walls, ceilings, or specific rooms where sensitive work is conducted. Shielding can also be used for devices, like placing **RF-blocking covers** on certain wireless devices to limit signal emissions.

Implementing RF-Blocking Technology in Workspaces

For offices dealing with sensitive information or those who want to provide employees with an RF-safe environment, implementing professional-grade RF-blocking technology is a more comprehensive solution. Below are some options for creating an RF-safe workspace:

1. Shielded Workstations

A shielded workstation is a dedicated space designed to block RF signals. These stations are usually built with **metal mesh panels** or **shielded enclosures** that reduce the level of RF radiation around the workspace. These can be installed in sensitive areas, such as **data centers**, **research facilities**, or places where confidential work is being done.

2. Shielded Rooms

For more significant RF protection, an entire **shielded room** or **Faraday room** can be constructed within the office. These rooms are completely enclosed by conductive materials (like **copper mesh** or **aluminum panels**) to block RF signals from entering or leaving the room. Shielded rooms are especially beneficial for employees working with confidential data or technology sensitive to RF interference.

3. RF-blocking Paint

For a more budget-friendly option, **RF-blocking paints** can be applied to walls, ceilings, or floors to prevent RF signals from entering or leaving rooms. These conductive paints are often made with **nickel** or **copper** and are suitable for small spaces or specific rooms that need RF shielding.

4. EMF-Reducing Furniture

Certain office furniture is designed with built-in **RF-blocking capabilities**. For example, desks, filing cabinets, or storage units with metalized panels or shielding material can help reduce RF exposure from devices placed within or on the furniture.

Legal Obligations and Workplace Safety Standards

Employers are legally required to provide a safe working environment for their employees, and this includes minimizing any potential hazards associated with RF exposure. In many countries, regulatory agencies have set standards and guidelines for limiting occupational exposure to electromagnetic fields (EMF), including RF radiation. These standards are outlined by organizations like the **Federal Communications Commission (FCC), Occupational Safety and Health Administration (OSHA)**, and the **International Commission on Non-Ionizing Radiation Protection (ICNIRP)**.

While specific standards vary by country, employers should be aware of the following:

- **Exposure Limits**: There are recommended limits on the amount of RF radiation an employee can be exposed to during their workday. For example, in the U.S., the **FCC** regulates the exposure limits for RF signals from devices like cellphones and routers to ensure they remain below harmful levels.
- **Risk Assessments**: Employers are encouraged to conduct **RF exposure risk assessments** in the workplace to identify areas of high exposure and take appropriate actions to reduce risk. This might involve implementing shielding solutions or adjusting the layout of devices.
- **Employee Training**: In workplaces where RF exposure is a concern, employers may need to provide training on how to manage and reduce exposure. This can include educating employees about how RF-emitting devices work, how to use shielding technology, and the potential health risks associated with prolonged exposure.

Conclusion

Reducing RF exposure in the workplace is a crucial step toward safeguarding the health, privacy, and productivity of employees. By implementing practical measures such as strategic router placement, wired connections, and managing Bluetooth usage, employees can mitigate their exposure to RF radiation. In more sensitive environments, professional-grade RF shielding solutions, such as shielded rooms and Faraday cages, offer additional protection. Furthermore, understanding the legal obligations surrounding RF exposure in the workplace ensures that employers create a safe and compliant working environment. Through these strategies, companies can effectively balance the need for connectivity with the responsibility to protect their employees from unnecessary RF exposure.

Chapter 13: RF Blocking for Personal Devices

Personal devices have become an integral part of our daily lives, from smartphones and tablets to laptops and wearable tech. These devices not only make communication and entertainment more accessible but also bring with them the constant transmission of Radio Frequency (RF) signals. These signals, while necessary for the functionality of these devices, raise concerns regarding privacy, health, and security. This chapter will explore how to protect yourself from the potential risks of RF radiation emitted by personal devices, the available RF-blocking products, and how to choose the right protection for your needs.

RF-Blocking Phone Cases and Accessories

One of the most common sources of RF exposure comes from smartphones. As modern phones connect to various networks (cellular, Wi-Fi, Bluetooth), they are continually emitting RF signals. This constant communication, especially when the device is in use, can result in prolonged exposure to RF radiation.

1. RF-Blocking Phone Cases

RF-blocking phone cases are specifically designed to reduce or eliminate the amount of radiation emitted by a phone. These cases typically incorporate materials like **copper**, **aluminum**, or **silver**, which are conductive metals known to reflect and absorb RF waves.

- **How They Work**: The phone case works by preventing the phone's RF signals from reaching the user's body. This is particularly useful for individuals who are concerned about constant, low-level exposure to radiation, especially during extended use. Some cases block all signals, including cellular, Wi-Fi, and Bluetooth, while others may only block specific types of signals.
- **Types of Cases**: There are different designs for RF-blocking phone cases, including full enclosures and partial shielding. Full enclosures wrap around the entire device, while partial cases focus on specific areas like the back or the sides of the phone. It's essential to assess which level of shielding is suitable for your needs.

2. RF-Blocking Pouches

RF-blocking pouches, often called **Faraday pouches**, are small bags lined with materials that block RF signals. These pouches are designed to block any RF signal emitted from a device inside the pouch, effectively turning off communication.

- **Use Cases**: These pouches are ideal for storing your phone when you want to disconnect and protect your data from potential tracking or remote access. They are also useful for preventing location tracking or hacking attempts, especially in public places or while traveling.
- **Convenience**: Unlike phone cases that need to be permanently attached to the phone, RF-blocking pouches can be used on demand, providing flexibility for when you want to block signals without needing to change your phone's setup permanently.

How to Use RF-Blocking Materials in Portable Devices

While smartphones and tablets are the primary devices of concern, other portable electronics such as laptops, e-readers, and portable gaming consoles also emit RF radiation. Using RF-blocking materials in these devices can help reduce overall exposure.

1. Laptop and Tablet Shields

Laptops and tablets emit RF radiation, especially when they are connected to Wi-Fi or Bluetooth. To reduce exposure, consider using **RF-blocking laptop sleeves** or **shields** that cover the device's wireless communication ports.

- **Laptop Shields**: These shields are usually made from materials like **conductive fabric** or **aluminum mesh**, which can block signals while still allowing the device to function. Some of these shields are designed to be used during periods of rest or transport, and they can be placed over the device to block signals when it's not in use.
- **Tablet Covers**: Similar to phone cases, RF-blocking tablet covers or cases work by creating a shield around the device, reducing RF radiation exposure when the device is in use. Many RF-blocking tablet covers are also made from **conductive fabrics** or **metal-infused** materials for maximum protection.

2. Portable RF-Blocking Devices

Portable **RF-blocking devices** can be attached to a variety of personal electronics, including e-readers, gaming consoles, and even smartwatches. These devices are designed to shield certain parts of your device, especially where RF signals are emitted.

- **RF-blocking Stickers**: These small adhesive stickers can be placed on the back of devices to block RF radiation in specific areas. The stickers are made from conductive materials and are designed to absorb or reflect RF signals, effectively reducing radiation exposure.
- **Clip-on Shields**: Similar to phone cases, some devices offer **clip-on shields** that can be attached to laptops, e-readers, and tablets to block RF waves. These shields are usually easy to install and remove, offering a simple solution for shielding without the need for bulky cases.

The Growing Market for RF-Blocking Tech

As awareness of RF radiation's potential risks increases, the demand for RF-blocking technology is growing. This has led to a burgeoning market for a variety of RF-blocking products, from phone cases to home shielding solutions. The RF-blocking tech market is still evolving, with innovations and new products emerging regularly.

1. RF-Blocking Fabrics and Clothing

The demand for wearable RF protection has led to the creation of **RF-blocking clothing**. These products are made from fabrics that contain woven metal fibers, such as **silver** or **copper**, designed to block RF signals from reaching the body.

- **Types of Clothing**: RF-blocking clothing includes **shirts, jackets, pants**, and **hats**. These can be particularly useful for individuals who are constantly exposed to RF signals in urban environments, offices, or while traveling. The clothing is often designed for comfort and style, making it an easy addition to daily attire.
- **Smart Fabrics**: Some innovative fabrics combine RF-blocking technology with other features, such as **anti-bacterial** properties or **temperature control**. These smart fabrics offer both health protection and comfort, making them an attractive option for the growing market of RF-aware consumers.

2. Home RF-Blocking Solutions

Many individuals are turning to home RF-blocking solutions to reduce their exposure during daily activities. These products can range from **RF-blocking window films** to **shielded rooms**.

- **RF-Blocking Window Films**: These films, often made from a combination of metal and film layers, are designed to block external RF signals while maintaining clear visibility. They can be applied to windows in homes or offices to minimize RF exposure from outside sources like cell towers or Wi-Fi signals.
- **Shielded Rooms**: More extreme measures, such as creating **shielded rooms** within homes or offices, are becoming popular among individuals who want to create RF-free zones. These rooms are equipped with **Faraday cages** or other RF-blocking materials to ensure complete isolation from RF radiation.

Choosing the Right Device for Your Needs

Selecting the appropriate RF-blocking device depends on your specific needs, lifestyle, and level of concern. Here are some factors to consider:

1. Level of Exposure

If you're concerned about low-level, continuous exposure, devices like **RF-blocking phone cases** and **portable shields** can help mitigate exposure during everyday use. For more significant exposure, such as from working near a Wi-Fi router or using a laptop for hours, more comprehensive shielding solutions like **laptop shields** or **RF-blocking sleeves** may be necessary.

2. Convenience vs. Protection

There is often a trade-off between convenience and protection. For instance, **RF-blocking pouches** offer an easy, portable solution, but you must remove your device from the pouch to use it. On the other hand, **full cases** offer continuous protection but can limit access to certain device functions. Consider your lifestyle and how much RF protection you are willing to sacrifice for convenience.

3. Budget

RF-blocking devices and accessories can vary widely in price. Basic solutions like **RF-blocking pouches** or **stickers** are generally affordable, while more advanced options, such as **shielded rooms** or **specialized clothing**, can be more expensive. Choose a solution that fits your budget and offers the level of protection you need.

Conclusion

RF-blocking technology for personal devices has become an essential consideration for those seeking to protect themselves from potential health and privacy risks associated with prolonged RF exposure. From **RF-blocking phone cases** and **portable pouches** to more advanced home shielding solutions, there are many options available to help reduce RF exposure in your daily life. As the market for these products continues to grow, so too will the variety of options available, making it easier for consumers to choose the right level of protection based on their needs and lifestyle.

Chapter 14: EMF and RF Testing

As awareness of the potential risks associated with electromagnetic fields (EMF) and radio frequency (RF) radiation grows, many individuals and organizations are seeking ways to measure and assess the levels of RF exposure in their environments. Understanding the levels of RF radiation around you is a critical step in making informed decisions about shielding and reducing exposure. This chapter provides an overview of how to measure RF levels, the tools and meters available for detecting RF signals, and how to interpret the readings to identify sources of interference. We'll also discuss how you can conduct your own RF safety assessments to ensure a healthier, more controlled environment.

How to Measure RF Levels in Your Environment

The first step in managing RF exposure is understanding how much RF radiation is present in your environment. While RF signals are often invisible and undetectable by the human senses, they can be measured using specialized tools designed to detect electromagnetic radiation. These measurements can help you assess the level of exposure from various sources and determine if shielding or mitigation is necessary.

1. RF Meters and Tools for Detecting RF Signals

There are several types of RF meters and tools available to measure the strength and frequency of RF signals. These tools vary in complexity and price, from basic handheld devices to more advanced systems used by professionals. Here's an overview of the most commonly used RF testing equipment:

Handheld RF Meters

electromagnetic field (EMF) strength

- **Pros**: Easy to use, affordable, and suitable for everyday users. They offer a quick and non-invasive way to measure RF exposure.
- **Cons**: These meters are less precise and may have limited frequency range compared to more advanced equipment.

Broadband RF Meters

- **Pros**: High accuracy and ability to measure a broader range of frequencies, including both high-frequency and low-frequency RF waves.
- **Cons**: More expensive and often more complicated to use than handheld meters.

Spectrum Analyzers

- **Pros**: Ideal for detailed RF studies, highly accurate, and capable of identifying specific frequency bands.
- **Cons**: Very expensive and typically requires technical expertise to operate effectively.

Smartphone Apps

- **Pros**: Convenient and cost-effective (often free or low-cost).
- **Cons**: Limited accuracy and range. Smartphones are not designed to detect RF radiation comprehensively.

2. Understanding RF Meters and Their Features

When choosing an RF meter, it is important to consider a few key features:

- **Frequency Range**: RF meters measure a range of frequencies, from **low frequencies (LF)** to **microwaves**. Different meters are designed to measure different parts of the electromagnetic spectrum, so it's essential to choose a meter that covers the specific frequencies of interest (e.g., Wi-Fi at 2.4 GHz and 5 GHz, cell phone signals, etc.).
- **Detection Sensitivity**: This refers to the minimum RF signal strength that the meter can detect. Meters with higher sensitivity will be able to detect weaker signals, making them more useful in environments with low RF exposure or for detecting devices that emit low power.
- **Display and Readout**: The ease of understanding the measurements is another important factor. Some meters offer simple numerical readouts, while others have more advanced features, like graphs or visual displays that show the intensity of the RF radiation.
- **Portability**: Consider the size and weight of the meter if you plan to move it around frequently. A lightweight, portable meter is easier to carry and use in various locations.

Interpreting RF Readings and Identifying Sources of Interference

Once you have an RF meter and have taken readings, the next step is to interpret the data. RF meters provide information about the intensity of the RF radiation, typically in **microwatts per square centimeter (µW/cm²)** or **volts per meter (V/m)**. Here's how to interpret these readings and understand the sources of RF interference:

1. Reading the Measurements

- **Low RF Levels (0-10 µW/cm²)**: These are generally considered safe and represent typical background levels of RF radiation in most environments.
- **Moderate RF Levels (10-50 µW/cm²)**: This range represents environments with higher RF exposure, which can occur in areas with several wireless devices, such as offices or homes with multiple Wi-Fi routers and cell phones.
- **High RF Levels (50+ µW/cm²)**: These levels are considered high and may pose a risk if exposure is prolonged. High levels may be found near strong RF sources like cell towers or high-powered transmitters.

2. Identifying Sources of RF Interference

Once the RF readings are taken, the next task is identifying the sources of RF radiation. Walk around the area with your RF meter to pinpoint areas with higher readings. Typical sources of interference include:

- **Wi-Fi Routers**: Wi-Fi routers are one of the most common sources of RF radiation in modern homes and offices. The RF levels typically peak near the router and decrease as you move further away.
- **Mobile Phones**: Cellphones emit RF radiation during calls, text messages, and internet use. The RF levels will fluctuate depending on whether the phone is actively transmitting data.
- **Bluetooth Devices**: Devices like Bluetooth speakers, wireless keyboards, and headsets emit RF signals, though typically at lower levels than Wi-Fi or mobile phones.
- **Microwave Ovens**: Microwave ovens can also emit RF radiation during use, although the levels are usually contained within the appliance's metal enclosure.

How to Conduct Your Own RF Safety Assessments

Conducting your own RF safety assessments allows you to take control of your exposure and identify areas where mitigation strategies may be necessary. Here's a step-by-step guide to performing an RF safety assessment:

1. Prepare Your Environment

Begin by ensuring that your RF meter is calibrated (if required) and ready for use. Clear any unnecessary clutter from the areas you plan to measure, and ensure that you have access to the devices you want to test (Wi-Fi router, mobile phones, etc.).

2. Measure RF Levels in Different Areas

Move through different rooms or areas of your home or office, taking measurements at various locations. Pay close attention to areas where you spend the most time, such as your work desk, bedroom, or living room. Record the readings for future reference.

3. Identify High-Risk Areas

Identify the areas where the RF levels are consistently high. These are typically places where many wireless devices are clustered together, such as near Wi-Fi routers, printers, or mobile phone charging stations. If any areas show excessive RF radiation levels, consider taking action to reduce exposure.

4. Take Action to Mitigate Exposure

Once you have identified areas with high RF exposure, take steps to mitigate it. This may involve relocating wireless devices, using RF-blocking materials like Faraday cages or shielding fabrics, or turning off devices when not in use. Consider using wired connections whenever possible to reduce the reliance on RF-emitting technologies.

5. Follow Up with Periodic Assessments

RF exposure levels can fluctuate over time as new devices are introduced into your environment or as devices are moved. Periodic assessments will allow you to track changes and ensure that your RF levels remain at safe levels.

Conclusion

RF and EMF testing provides a practical way to assess your exposure to potentially harmful radiation and identify the sources of RF interference in your environment. By using the right tools, interpreting the readings correctly, and taking appropriate action to reduce exposure, you can create a safer, healthier environment for yourself and your family. Regular RF testing empowers you to take control of your exposure levels and ensures that your decisions about RF shielding and protection are based on data rather than assumptions.

Chapter 15: The Legal Landscape of RF Blocking

As concerns about the potential risks of RF (Radio Frequency) exposure continue to grow, it is essential to understand the legal landscape surrounding RF blocking and shielding. While RF radiation is part of daily life, there are various regulations and standards in place to manage and mitigate its effects. These regulations often vary by country, but they share a common goal: to protect public health while allowing for the continued use of RF technology.

This chapter provides an overview of the key regulatory bodies involved in managing RF exposure, the legal concerns surrounding RF shielding and blocking, and the implications of intellectual property and patents related to RF technology.

Understanding Regulations Around RF Blocking

The regulation of RF radiation is primarily concerned with controlling exposure to electromagnetic fields (EMFs) to prevent harmful health effects. Different organizations around the world set standards for RF exposure, taking into account scientific research on potential risks and health impacts.

1. Government Agencies and Standards

Several government agencies are responsible for regulating RF exposure and ensuring that products emitting RF radiation meet safety standards. Key players include:

- **Federal Communications Commission (FCC) (United States)**: The FCC plays a central role in regulating RF emissions in the U.S., particularly concerning telecommunications and broadcasting. The FCC sets limits on the amount of RF radiation that can be emitted by devices such as cell phones, radios, and microwave ovens. These regulations are designed to protect the public from harmful exposure while allowing for technological advancements. The FCC also enforces rules on radio spectrum use, ensuring that RF signals from various devices do not interfere with one another.

- **Environmental Protection Agency (EPA) (United States)**: The EPA provides guidelines on environmental exposure to RF radiation and oversees studies on the potential health impacts of EMF and RF fields. While the EPA does not set specific limits on RF exposure, it plays a vital role in public health research and informs policy decisions related to RF safety.

- **International Commission on Non-Ionizing Radiation Protection (ICNIRP)**: The ICNIRP is an international body that provides guidelines on safe levels of non-ionizing radiation, including RF and electromagnetic fields. The organization's guidelines are widely adopted by various countries and are often used as a benchmark for setting national safety standards.

- **World Health Organization (WHO)**: The WHO provides recommendations and reports on RF radiation and its potential health effects. It has stated that, based on current evidence, RF radiation does not cause adverse health effects at the levels commonly encountered by the general public. However, the WHO continues to monitor ongoing research into the effects of long-term exposure.
- **European Union (EU)**: The EU has developed specific regulations regarding the protection of workers and the general public from RF radiation. These regulations apply to various industries, including telecommunications and broadcasting. The EU also funds research into the health effects of RF radiation and supports international efforts to standardize exposure limits.

2. Exposure Limits and Safety Guidelines

Exposure limits for RF radiation are designed to prevent harmful biological effects, such as tissue damage or thermal effects caused by intense exposure. These limits are based on the frequency and intensity of RF radiation and are typically set to ensure the safety of individuals who use wireless devices or work in environments with high RF exposure.

- **Specific Absorption Rate (SAR)**: The SAR is a measure of the rate at which energy is absorbed by the body when exposed to an RF field. The SAR is commonly used to regulate the radiation emitted by mobile phones. The FCC sets limits for SAR levels, ensuring that the amount of RF energy absorbed by the body remains below a certain threshold.

- **Exposure Thresholds**: Regulatory agencies around the world, including the FCC and ICNIRP, have established specific thresholds for RF exposure. These thresholds vary by frequency and are based on extensive research into the potential health effects of RF radiation. For instance, the recommended exposure limit for the general public is usually lower than that for workers who are exposed to RF fields in occupational settings.

While regulatory bodies continue to monitor and update these standards based on new scientific data, there remains ongoing debate over the long-term effects of RF exposure, especially at lower levels over extended periods. This has led to calls for stricter regulations and more research into the cumulative effects of RF radiation.

Legal Concerns Around RF Shielding and Blocking

As concerns over RF radiation grow, many individuals and businesses are turning to RF shielding as a way to protect themselves from potential harm. However, this raises important legal and regulatory questions regarding the use and development of RF-blocking technologies.

1. RF Shielding in the Marketplace

The demand for RF-blocking products, including shielding materials and personal devices, has led to an expanding market of products designed to mitigate exposure. These products range from **RF-blocking fabrics** used in clothing and home furnishings to **Faraday cages** and **RF-blocking phone cases**. While these products can provide substantial protection from RF radiation, there are several legal considerations that manufacturers and consumers must be aware of.

- **Product Claims and Advertising**: One of the key legal concerns related to RF-blocking products is the accuracy of product claims. Manufacturers must ensure that their products do not make misleading claims about the level of protection they offer. For instance, a phone case marketed as "100% RF-blocking" may be misleading if it only reduces RF exposure by a small percentage or blocks certain types of signals but not others. Regulatory bodies may scrutinize these claims, and manufacturers could face penalties for deceptive advertising practices.
- **Certification and Testing**: Many RF-blocking products are sold without formal certification or third-party testing, leading to concerns about their effectiveness. In some jurisdictions, manufacturers may be required to submit their products for testing and certification to ensure they meet certain standards for RF blocking. In the U.S., for example, products that claim to block RF radiation may need to comply with the FCC's standards for consumer electronics.

- **Patents and Intellectual Property**: The development of RF-blocking technologies has led to a rise in intellectual property (IP) issues. As companies innovate in the field of RF shielding, patents are increasingly being filed for new materials and devices that offer enhanced protection from RF radiation. Businesses in this field must be mindful of patent infringement risks and ensure that their products do not violate existing patents. Conversely, inventors and companies creating new RF-blocking technologies must protect their innovations through patents to prevent unauthorized use of their ideas.

2. Legal Challenges in Implementing RF Shielding

RF shielding technologies can face challenges when it comes to practical implementation, particularly in public or commercial spaces. In some cases, RF-blocking materials may interfere with essential services, such as telecommunications or emergency communications, raising potential conflicts with regulatory authorities.

- **Building Codes and Infrastructure**: In certain jurisdictions, there are building codes that mandate the inclusion of wireless infrastructure, such as Wi-Fi networks, cell signal boosters, and public communication systems. These regulations may limit the extent to which individuals or organizations can shield their environments from RF radiation. For instance, if a business wants to create an RF-free zone, it may face resistance from local authorities if it interferes with municipal wireless systems or emergency communication networks.
- **Public and Workplace Safety**: In workplace environments, RF shielding solutions must balance personal safety with legal requirements for communication systems. Employers are required to ensure that their employees' safety is not compromised by excessive RF exposure, but they must also ensure that RF-blocking materials do not interfere with essential wireless communication devices used for business operations.

Intellectual Property and Patents in RF Technology

The RF-blocking technology market has seen significant innovation, leading to the development of new materials and devices designed to protect individuals from RF radiation. As with any emerging technology, intellectual property (IP) issues are a key concern for companies and inventors.

- **Patent Protection for Innovations**: Companies in the RF-blocking space need to protect their intellectual property by filing patents for innovative shielding materials or devices. Patents ensure that inventors and companies have exclusive rights to their technologies and can prevent competitors from copying their designs.
- **Patent Infringement Risks**: As the market for RF-blocking products grows, the potential for patent infringement increases. Companies developing new shielding technologies must conduct thorough patent searches to ensure their innovations do not violate existing patents. Failure to do so could result in costly legal battles and the loss of intellectual property rights.

Conclusion

Navigating the legal landscape surrounding RF blocking requires understanding the various regulations and standards governing RF exposure and shielding technologies. As the demand for RF-blocking products continues to rise, manufacturers must be mindful of legal issues such as product claims, certification, and intellectual property. At the same time, consumers and businesses must ensure that they comply with regulations and consider the broader implications of implementing RF shielding in their environments. By staying informed about legal developments and respecting existing regulations, individuals can safely incorporate RF-blocking technologies into their lives while protecting their health and privacy.

Chapter 16: Innovations in RF Blocking Technologies

As society becomes increasingly aware of the potential risks associated with RF (Radio Frequency) exposure, the demand for innovative RF blocking solutions continues to grow. Technology is constantly evolving, and so are the methods and materials used to mitigate RF radiation. This chapter explores the latest advancements in RF blocking technologies, including the role of artificial intelligence (AI) and machine learning in managing RF waves, the evolution of shielding materials, and emerging trends in RF wave protection. It also discusses how future research and development will continue to shape the landscape of RF blocking.

Emerging Technologies and Future Trends

RF blocking technology is an evolving field, driven by the need for better, more effective methods of shielding from harmful RF radiation. New technologies are enabling more advanced and efficient ways to protect against RF exposure while maintaining functionality and convenience. Here are some of the most promising emerging technologies:

1. AI and Machine Learning for RF Wave Management

Artificial intelligence (AI) and machine learning are beginning to play a significant role in the management of RF waves. By analyzing large volumes of data from RF meters and other sensing devices, AI can help optimize RF shielding and predict areas of high exposure.

- **Predictive Shielding**: AI can be used to analyze RF signal patterns and predict areas of high exposure within a given environment. This allows for the proactive deployment of RF-blocking materials or devices in the areas most likely to receive high levels of RF radiation. AI can also dynamically adjust shielding levels based on the intensity and frequency of the RF signals detected, providing a more responsive and tailored solution to RF management.
- **Machine Learning in Device Design**: In the future, machine learning could be used to design more efficient RF-blocking devices. By analyzing how RF signals interact with different materials, algorithms could be developed to optimize the placement, thickness, and material properties of shielding devices. This would lead to more effective products that offer a higher degree of protection without compromising convenience or style.

2. Smart RF-Blocking Materials

The development of smart materials capable of blocking RF waves has the potential to revolutionize RF shielding technology. These materials can automatically respond to changes in the RF environment and adjust their properties accordingly.

- **Self-Regulating Shielding**: Smart RF-blocking materials can adapt in real-time to varying levels of RF radiation. For example, materials embedded with **nano-scale sensors** could detect changes in RF exposure and alter their electromagnetic properties to increase shielding when necessary. These materials could be used in various applications, including wearable devices, building materials, and personal shielding items.
- **Transparent Conductive Films**: One of the challenges with traditional RF-blocking materials is that they often sacrifice aesthetics for function. Transparent conductive films are a new development that allows for RF shielding without compromising visibility or light transmission. These films can be applied to windows, walls, or even smartphones to block RF signals while still allowing users to enjoy natural light or clear displays.

3. RF-Blocking Wearables

As wearable technology continues to grow in popularity, innovative RF-blocking wearables are being developed to protect users from constant RF exposure. These wearables are designed to block RF signals from smartphones, Wi-Fi routers, and other sources of radiation while allowing users to continue their daily activities.

- **RF-Blocking Clothing**: RF-blocking clothing is one of the most promising innovations in personal protection. This includes garments such as **jackets**, **pants**, **hats**, and **gloves** that integrate conductive materials like **copper**, **silver**, or **nickel** into the fabric. These materials block or absorb RF signals, providing protection without the need for bulky devices.
- **RF-Blocking Jewelry**: In addition to clothing, jewelry and accessories like **bracelets**, **necklaces**, and **earrings** are being designed with RF-blocking properties. These wearable devices are often crafted with special materials that shield the body from RF waves while offering stylish, everyday wear. This allows individuals to protect themselves without compromising fashion or comfort.

4. Portable RF Shielding Devices

There has been a growing interest in portable RF shielding devices, particularly for people who are constantly on the move. These devices are designed to create a protective barrier against RF radiation in specific environments, such as public spaces, offices, or even while traveling.

- **Portable Faraday Bags**: Faraday bags, which block RF signals, are becoming more sophisticated and user-friendly. These bags, which were once primarily used for protecting electronics during travel, now come in a variety of sizes and designs, offering protection for phones, laptops, and other personal devices. New innovations allow these bags to be lighter, more flexible, and easier to carry, making them an ideal solution for individuals seeking portable RF protection.
- **RF-Blocking Shields for Public Spaces**: In public spaces like airports, coffee shops, and libraries, RF-blocking shields can be placed around workstations or seating areas to create an RF-free zone. These shields use materials like **conductive fabrics** or **Faraday cages** to block incoming RF signals from mobile phones, Wi-Fi routers, and other sources, providing a temporary safe space for individuals who wish to minimize their exposure to RF radiation.

The Evolution of RF-Blocking Materials

RF-blocking materials have come a long way since the first rudimentary shields were introduced. Early RF-blocking materials were typically heavy, rigid, and difficult to apply, but advances in materials science have led to the development of lighter, more flexible, and more effective solutions. Here are some notable advancements:

1. Advanced Conductive Fabrics

Conductive fabrics have been a key innovation in RF shielding. These fabrics are woven with conductive metals like **copper**, **silver**, or **nickel** and are used in a variety of applications, from wearable technology to building materials. The fabrics are lightweight, breathable, and flexible, making them easy to integrate into clothing, curtains, and other everyday items.

New Composite Materials

2. Graphene-Based Materials

Graphene, a material made from a single layer of carbon atoms arranged in a honeycomb structure, is being explored as an advanced material for RF shielding. Graphene has remarkable electrical conductivity and flexibility, making it an ideal candidate for developing thin, lightweight RF-blocking materials.

Potential Applications

3. High-Performance Faraday Cages

Faraday cages are well-known for their ability to block electromagnetic radiation, but new innovations are making them more effective and easier to use. Advanced Faraday cages are now being built with lighter, more durable materials that are easier to install in homes, offices, and even portable enclosures.

Modular Faraday Cages

modular Faraday cages

Future Research and Development in RF Wave Protection

Research in RF wave protection continues to advance, with scientists and engineers exploring new materials, technologies, and methods to better shield individuals from harmful RF radiation. As we learn more about the long-term effects of RF exposure, new solutions will emerge to address these risks.

- **Biocompatible Shielding**: One area of future research involves developing RF-blocking materials that are not only effective but also biocompatible. These materials would be safe for long-term use in contact with the skin and would be suitable for products like wearable technology, personal accessories, and even implants.
- **RF-Free Communication**: As the world moves toward safer communication technologies, future innovations may include new forms of **wireless communication** that use lower energy levels and produce less RF radiation. Researchers are exploring alternative communication methods, such as **quantum communication**, that could one day replace current wireless technologies, reducing the need for RF-emitting devices.

Conclusion

Innovations in RF-blocking technologies are progressing rapidly, offering more effective and convenient ways to protect individuals from the potential risks associated with RF radiation. From AI-powered RF management systems to advanced materials like graphene and conductive fabrics, the future of RF blocking is bright. As new technologies emerge, individuals will have access to even better ways to shield themselves from RF exposure while maintaining connectivity and convenience. With ongoing research and development, the promise of safer communication solutions is on the horizon, ensuring that the world of tomorrow is healthier and more connected.

Chapter 17: The Global Perspective on RF Waves

In a world where technology is advancing rapidly, the issue of radio frequency (RF) exposure has garnered global attention. Different countries have varying approaches to managing RF radiation, creating a diverse landscape of standards, regulations, and cultural attitudes toward wireless technology. Understanding these international perspectives on RF waves is crucial for individuals, businesses, and governments alike, as the debate about how to manage RF exposure becomes a global conversation.

This chapter explores how various nations handle RF exposure, the international standards for RF protection, cultural attitudes toward RF blocking, and how global health and environmental policies shape the regulation of RF technologies.

How Different Countries Handle RF Exposure

Regulating RF exposure is a complex task that involves balancing technological progress with the need to safeguard public health. Different countries approach this challenge in unique ways, influenced by scientific research, public health concerns, and technological needs. Here are some examples of how RF exposure is managed worldwide:

1. United States

In the U.S., RF exposure is regulated by several agencies, including the **Federal Communications Commission (FCC)** and the **Environmental Protection Agency (EPA)**. The FCC sets guidelines for RF emissions from telecommunications devices, such as cell phones, radio transmitters, and Wi-Fi routers. These guidelines are based on a limit for **Specific Absorption Rate (SAR)**, which measures the rate at which the human body absorbs RF energy.

- The **FCC's guidelines** are among the most recognized in the world, establishing safe exposure limits for RF radiation, although concerns over long-term health effects continue to fuel debate among experts and advocacy groups.
- The **EPA** monitors environmental RF radiation and funds research into the potential health effects of RF exposure. It does not establish specific exposure limits, but it provides recommendations on minimizing exposure, particularly in residential settings.

2. European Union

The European Union (EU) has its own regulations regarding RF exposure, which are similar in many ways to those in the U.S. However, EU regulations are influenced by the **International Commission on Non-Ionizing Radiation Protection (ICNIRP)**, which provides exposure guidelines for non-ionizing radiation (including RF and electromagnetic fields).

- The **ICNIRP guidelines** are widely adopted across Europe and set limits on RF exposure to prevent health risks. These guidelines focus on thermal effects (such as heating of body tissues) and ensure that RF exposure levels remain below thresholds considered harmful.
- European countries have also taken steps to regulate the use of mobile phones and wireless technology in schools, particularly for younger children. Some countries, such as France and Germany, have adopted stricter regulations to limit RF exposure to minors.

3. China

China is one of the largest markets for mobile technology and wireless communication, and it has implemented its own set of RF exposure regulations. The country follows the guidelines set by the **World Health Organization (WHO)** and the **ICNIRP** to establish safe RF exposure limits.

- **China's Ministry of Industry and Information Technology (MIIT)** is responsible for regulating wireless communication equipment and monitoring RF exposure from devices like mobile phones and base stations.
- China has also adopted safety standards for wireless communication devices, ensuring that devices sold in the country comply with national RF safety requirements. However, concerns about the long-term health effects of RF exposure persist, and research into these effects continues.

4. India

India has been proactive in addressing concerns related to RF radiation from mobile phones and telecom towers. The country follows the RF exposure guidelines set by the **ICNIRP** and the **WHO**, and its **Department of Telecommunications (DoT)** has issued guidelines for mobile service providers to ensure compliance with safe exposure levels.

- India has also taken steps to reduce public exposure to RF radiation by setting limits on the power levels emitted by mobile towers and regulating the placement of towers near residential areas.
- In 2012, India introduced a **mobile tower radiation norm** that set stricter limits on RF emissions from mobile towers to reduce exposure to residents. These efforts are part of India's commitment to balancing the growth of telecommunications infrastructure with public health and safety.

5. Australia

Australia's regulations for RF exposure are largely influenced by the **Australian Radiation Protection and Nuclear Safety Agency (ARPANSA)**, which provides guidance on minimizing exposure to RF radiation. The agency follows the ICNIRP's guidelines and ensures that RF exposure from telecommunications and other wireless technologies is within safe limits.

- **ARPANSA** conducts regular monitoring of RF radiation levels across the country, especially in areas with high concentrations of mobile towers, radio transmitters, and Wi-Fi networks. Public awareness campaigns are also conducted to educate citizens on minimizing unnecessary RF exposure.
- Australia has also been active in investigating the potential health risks of prolonged RF exposure, with a focus on the effects of mobile phone use on children and young adults.

International Standards for RF Protection

While individual countries set their own limits for RF exposure, there is significant international cooperation in establishing standardized guidelines. Two key organizations that shape global RF protection standards are the **International Commission on Non-Ionizing Radiation Protection (ICNIRP)** and the **World Health Organization (WHO)**.

1. International Commission on Non-Ionizing Radiation Protection (ICNIRP)

The ICNIRP is an independent organization that provides global guidelines for non-ionizing radiation, including RF exposure. Its recommendations are adopted by many countries and form the basis of regulations set by national agencies, such as the FCC in the U.S. and ARPANSA in Australia.

- The **ICNIRP's guidelines** are based on current scientific evidence regarding the potential health effects of RF radiation. The organization focuses on the thermal effects of RF radiation, which can cause tissue damage, and sets limits to prevent this type of harm.
- The ICNIRP's guidelines are regularly updated to reflect the latest research on RF radiation and its potential effects on health. While there is broad agreement on the safety of RF exposure within established limits, ongoing research continues to explore potential non-thermal effects, such as impacts on the brain or DNA.

2. World Health Organization (WHO)

The WHO plays a significant role in global health policy related to RF exposure, with a particular focus on scientific research and public education. The organization monitors emerging health data related to RF radiation and provides advice to governments on managing exposure.

The WHO's

has classified RF radiation as possibly carcinogenic to humans (Group 2B), based on limited evidence that it may increase the risk of cancer. However, the agency maintains that there is no conclusive evidence that RF radiation from mobile phones causes cancer, and it continues to support further research into the potential long-term effects of exposure.

3. Other Organizations

In addition to the ICNIRP and WHO, several other organizations contribute to global standards for RF exposure. These include:

- The **European Union (EU)**, which follows ICNIRP guidelines and works with national regulatory bodies to ensure RF exposure is within safe limits.
- The **International Telecommunication Union (ITU)**, which coordinates global standards for telecommunications and radio spectrum management, ensuring that wireless technologies operate within safe RF limits and that interference between RF signals is minimized.

Cultural Attitudes Toward RF Blocking

Cultural attitudes toward RF blocking and RF exposure vary significantly from country to country. In some nations, there is a strong public push for reducing RF exposure due to health concerns, while in others, there is a greater focus on technological advancement and economic growth.

1. Proactive Nations (France, Germany)

Countries like **France** and **Germany** have taken a more proactive stance in regulating RF radiation, particularly regarding the use of mobile phones and Wi-Fi in schools and public spaces. These nations have stricter regulations on mobile phone emissions and have introduced initiatives to raise awareness about the potential risks of RF radiation.

- **France** has been particularly vocal about reducing RF exposure, introducing laws that restrict the use of Wi-Fi in schools and requiring mobile phones to display radiation levels.
- **Germany** also encourages the use of landlines over mobile phones, particularly for children, and provides recommendations on how to minimize RF exposure in the home.

2. Technologically-Oriented Countries (U.S., Japan, South Korea)

In countries like the **U.S.**, **Japan**, and **South Korea**, the focus tends to be more on technological innovation and ensuring the continued growth of the telecommunications industry. While these nations recognize the importance of RF safety, there is generally less public concern about RF exposure.

These countries have established regulatory frameworks to ensure that RF radiation levels from devices like mobile phones and base stations remain within safe limits. However, the conversation about long-term health risks is less prominent compared to countries with stricter regulations.

Global Health and Environmental Policies

RF exposure regulation is not just about public health but also involves environmental concerns. As mobile technology spreads across the globe, especially in developing countries, there is an increasing focus on the environmental impact of RF radiation. This includes the potential effects on wildlife, plant life, and the broader ecosystem.

- The **World Health Organization** and other environmental agencies continue to assess the environmental impact of RF radiation, particularly the effects of mobile towers and base stations on surrounding wildlife.
- Some countries have enacted regulations to minimize the environmental impact of RF radiation, including rules on the placement of mobile towers and base stations in ecologically sensitive areas.

Conclusion

The global perspective on RF waves reveals a complex and diverse approach to managing RF exposure. While countries like the U.S. and Japan focus on technological advancement and economic growth, nations in Europe and parts of Asia have adopted more precautionary measures to reduce RF radiation and its potential health impacts. As the science behind RF exposure continues to evolve, international standards and local regulations will continue to play a critical role in ensuring public health and safety in the digital age. Understanding these global perspectives helps individuals and businesses navigate the landscape of RF radiation, ultimately empowering them to make informed decisions about their health, privacy, and environment.

Chapter 18: The Psychological Effects of Disconnecting

In our increasingly connected world, where smartphones, laptops, and wireless networks dominate our daily lives, the ability to disconnect has become an essential aspect of maintaining mental and emotional well-being. While much focus has been placed on the physical effects of RF (radio frequency) exposure, there is a growing body of research that suggests reducing exposure to RF waves may also offer significant psychological benefits. This chapter explores the mental health advantages of reducing RF exposure, the concept of a digital detox, and the societal shifts that are encouraging tech-free zones and lifestyles that promote well-being.

The Mental Health Benefits of Reducing RF Exposure

While the direct psychological impacts of RF exposure are still under investigation, several indirect factors suggest that reducing exposure could improve mental health. Much of this has to do with the stress associated with constant connectivity, and the role that RF-emitting devices play in keeping us engaged in a hyper-connected world.

1. Decreased Stress and Anxiety

Smartphones and constant connectivity have become significant contributors to stress and anxiety. The perpetual bombardment of notifications, emails, and alerts creates a sense of urgency and pressure, leading to higher levels of cortisol (the stress hormone). When exposed to RF radiation, the body can experience increased stress, although the precise mechanisms are still being studied. However, the mental strain caused by always being "on" is well-documented.

Reducing exposure to RF signals, such as by switching off devices or spending time in RF-free environments, can help reduce this constant pressure. People who practice regular "digital detoxes" or limit their screen time often report feeling more relaxed, less stressed, and more mentally refreshed.

2. Improved Sleep Quality

One of the most significant mental health benefits of disconnecting from RF waves is improved sleep quality. RF radiation, particularly from mobile phones, Wi-Fi routers, and other wireless devices, has been associated with sleep disturbances. Electromagnetic fields (EMFs) have been shown in some studies to disrupt circadian rhythms, the natural sleep-wake cycle, which can negatively affect sleep.

Research suggests that spending time away from RF-emitting devices, especially before bedtime, can help improve sleep quality, leading to better mental health outcomes. People who reduce their exposure to RF sources report falling asleep faster, experiencing deeper sleep, and waking up feeling more rested.

3. Reduced Cognitive Overload

In today's world, constant engagement with digital devices can lead to cognitive overload, a state in which the brain is overstimulated and unable to process information effectively. RF radiation contributes to this phenomenon as wireless signals are constantly processed by devices, leading to mental fatigue.

Disconnecting from RF signals, such as taking breaks from smartphones, can provide the brain with the necessary downtime to reset. Studies have shown that when individuals take time away from screens and wireless devices, they experience improved concentration, better decision-making, and heightened cognitive clarity.

Digital Detox and the Impact of Less RF Communication

A digital detox refers to intentionally disconnecting from all forms of technology, particularly wireless devices, for a set period. The digital detox trend has gained significant traction in recent years, as people become increasingly aware of the negative psychological effects of overuse of digital devices, including smartphones, computers, and tablets.

1. Reducing Digital Dependence

Constant connection to RF-emitting devices, such as smartphones and computers, often leads to a dependence on technology for information, social interaction, and even entertainment. This digital dependence can be overwhelming, creating feelings of inadequacy, insecurity, or even loneliness, as people become fixated on online interactions rather than real-world experiences.

Taking breaks from technology or committing to a digital detox can help people regain a sense of control and reduce their reliance on technology for emotional fulfillment. By disconnecting from digital devices, individuals can reconnect with their environment, loved ones, and their own thoughts, which can significantly improve mental well-being.

2. Rebalancing Social Interactions

The digital age has also altered how we interact with others. While online communication offers convenience, it can often feel impersonal, leading to feelings of isolation despite being more "connected." Social media, for example, often fosters a sense of disconnection rather than connection, as it can amplify feelings of comparison, jealousy, and inadequacy.

Digital detoxes, especially in social media contexts, allow individuals to regain a sense of authentic connection by focusing on face-to-face interactions. Reducing exposure to social media platforms can reduce feelings of anxiety and loneliness, while improving social satisfaction and emotional support.

The Rise of Tech-Free Zones and Lifestyle Choices

In recent years, there has been a growing movement to create tech-free zones in both personal and public spaces, where people intentionally disconnect from technology to prioritize mental and emotional well-being. These spaces can vary from private homes to public parks, offices, and even cafes.

1. Tech-Free Zones in Homes and Offices

More individuals and businesses are creating tech-free zones within their homes or workplaces as part of a broader effort to manage RF exposure and reduce distractions. In a home, a tech-free zone may include a designated room or area where phones, tablets, and laptops are not allowed, helping to foster relaxation and family connection.

Office settings

2. Public Spaces Promoting Disconnecting

In cities and communities, some public spaces are encouraging "tech-free" hours or sections, where visitors are encouraged to leave their devices at home or turn them off during their visit. This can include public parks, libraries, or museums that promote RF-free environments. These spaces offer a chance to engage with nature, art, or literature without the distractions of wireless technology.

Public campaigns, such as "unplug to reconnect" initiatives, are gaining traction. These programs are designed to encourage people to take time off from their devices to enjoy mindful activities, such as reading, walking, or simply sitting in nature, all while minimizing RF exposure.

Social Implications of Reduced Connectivity

Disconnecting from RF communication, while beneficial for individual health, also has broader social implications. As more people embrace the benefits of reduced connectivity, societal attitudes toward constant digital engagement are shifting.

1. Promoting Balance Over Extremes

In a world dominated by constant digital stimulation, the movement toward disconnecting from RF waves advocates for a more balanced approach to technology use. Rather than rejecting technology entirely, the goal is to use it mindfully and in moderation, ensuring that it enhances rather than hinders personal and social well-being.

A societal shift is underway that emphasizes the importance of balancing connectivity with the need for personal space and quiet. This includes recognizing the value of face-to-face communication, fostering community engagement, and creating environments where technology does not dominate every aspect of daily life.

2. Building a Mindful Digital Culture

As more individuals and organizations adopt practices like digital detoxes and tech-free zones, there is a growing cultural awareness of the need to preserve human connection in an increasingly digital world. A mindful digital culture focuses on intentional use of technology, with an emphasis on well-being, privacy, and human connection.

This culture encourages people to be conscious of their technology use, setting boundaries that allow for meaningful offline experiences, personal growth, and healthier relationships. With this approach, individuals can strike a balance between staying connected and protecting their mental health.

Conclusion

Reducing RF exposure by disconnecting from wireless technologies has far-reaching psychological benefits. From decreasing stress and improving sleep quality to fostering authentic social interactions, disconnecting from RF communication helps restore balance in an over-connected world. Embracing digital detoxes and creating tech-free zones not only enhances personal well-being but also promotes a cultural shift toward mindful technology use. As we continue to navigate the digital age, understanding the psychological effects of disconnecting and integrating healthier, more intentional technology habits will be essential to maintaining our mental health in the years to come.

Chapter 19: Building an RF-Free Zone

As awareness of the potential risks of radio frequency (RF) exposure continues to grow, many individuals are choosing to create RF-free zones in their homes, workplaces, and other environments. These spaces allow for a respite from the constant bombardment of RF radiation, offering an opportunity to improve health, well-being, and focus. In this chapter, we will explore how to create an RF-free environment, the steps to plan such a space for optimal RF blocking, and how to design RF-free zones in both personal and public areas. We will also look at case studies of successful RF-free zones, offering inspiration for your own journey toward a safer, more balanced life.

Steps to Create an RF-Free Environment

Creating an RF-free zone requires intentional planning, strategic shielding, and consistent maintenance. Whether you are designing a completely RF-free space in your home or office, or just looking to reduce exposure in certain areas, there are several key steps to follow.

1. Assess the Current RF Environment

Before you can begin creating an RF-free zone, it's important to understand the current level of RF exposure in the area. This will help you identify the sources of RF radiation and determine how to shield or block them effectively.

- **Use an RF meter**: A handheld RF meter or electromagnetic field (EMF) tester can help you measure the strength and frequency of RF radiation in the environment. These meters are widely available and can be used to identify hotspots where RF exposure is high. This will allow you to pinpoint the most critical areas for shielding.
- **Map out RF sources**: Common sources of RF exposure include mobile phones, Wi-Fi routers, microwaves, baby monitors, smart home devices, and wireless computers. Make a list of all devices that emit RF waves, and determine which ones are necessary and which can be turned off or replaced with wired alternatives.

2. Define Your RF-Free Zones

After assessing the current environment, the next step is to define the areas where you want to create an RF-free zone. The goal is to minimize RF exposure in the areas where you spend the most time, such as bedrooms, home offices, or relaxation spaces.

- **Bedrooms**: Since sleep quality can be significantly impacted by RF exposure, many people choose to make their bedrooms RF-free zones. To do this, remove or turn off devices that emit RF radiation during the night, such as cell phones, Wi-Fi routers, and smart speakers.
- **Workspaces**: If you work from home, consider creating a tech-free office or study area. This space should be dedicated to focused work without distractions from wireless signals. If your office requires internet access, consider using wired Ethernet connections rather than relying on Wi-Fi.
- **Living Areas**: Common areas, like living rooms and kitchens, may still need to accommodate technology. However, you can reduce RF exposure by turning off devices when not in use or placing them away from sitting areas.

3. Implement RF Shielding Solutions

Once you have identified the RF-free zones, the next step is to implement shielding solutions to block or absorb RF waves. There are various options for shielding, depending on the space and the level of protection you need.

- **Faraday Cages**: A Faraday cage is a protective enclosure made of conductive material that blocks RF waves. For smaller spaces, such as a home office or bedroom, you can create a DIY Faraday cage by lining the walls with conductive fabric or mesh. This will block incoming and outgoing RF signals, ensuring that the space remains RF-free.
- **Conductive Fabrics and Mesh**: For areas where a Faraday cage might not be practical, conductive fabrics and meshes are an excellent solution. These materials can be applied to windows, walls, or even curtains to shield against RF radiation. Look for fabrics made from copper, silver, or other conductive metals, as these are highly effective at blocking RF waves.
- **RF-Blocking Paint**: Special RF-blocking paints are available that can be applied to walls and ceilings to reduce RF exposure. These paints contain conductive materials, such as carbon or graphite, that form a shield against RF waves. This can be especially useful in creating a shielded bedroom or office.
- **Shielding Paint for Windows**: Windows are often a significant source of RF exposure, especially in urban environments where signals are strong. There are specific shielding films and paints available for windows that reduce RF radiation while still allowing light to enter the space.

4. Replace Wireless Technology with Wired Alternatives

One of the simplest ways to reduce RF exposure is to replace wireless devices with wired alternatives wherever possible.

- **Ethernet Over Wi-Fi**: Wi-Fi routers emit RF radiation constantly, even when you're not using the internet. By switching to a wired Ethernet connection, you can eliminate the need for wireless signals. Use Ethernet cables to connect devices like computers, printers, and gaming consoles, ensuring they no longer rely on Wi-Fi.
- **Landline Phones**: Replace wireless or cell phones with traditional landline phones that do not emit RF radiation. This simple switch can reduce the RF exposure in your home or office while maintaining communication.
- **Wired Peripherals**: Use wired keyboards, mice, and other peripherals to reduce reliance on Bluetooth and other RF-based technologies.

5. Establish Technology-Free Zones

In addition to creating RF-free areas, you may want to designate technology-free zones for activities like relaxation, sleep, and meals. These spaces encourage you to disconnect from digital devices and enjoy moments of calm and mindfulness.

- **Tech-Free Living Rooms and Dining Areas**: Designate spaces where no devices are allowed. Create a designated "unplugged" zone for meals or family time, where everyone can engage without distractions from smartphones, tablets, or laptops.
- **Outdoor Spaces**: If you have a garden or balcony, it can serve as an excellent RF-free zone where you can enjoy nature without interference from electronic devices. Opt for activities that engage your senses, like reading or gardening, without the need for digital distractions.

Case Studies of Successful RF-Free Zones

1. The Tech-Free Home in California

In California, a family of four decided to turn their home into an RF-free sanctuary after learning about the potential health risks of constant exposure. They implemented a combination of Faraday cages and conductive fabrics in the bedrooms and created a tech-free zone in the living room. The results were immediate—improved sleep quality, reduced stress levels, and enhanced family communication. They also found that their children's focus and creativity improved as a result of reduced screen time.

2. The RF-Free Office in Sweden

A tech company in Sweden took steps to reduce RF exposure in their workplace by installing Faraday shielding materials in their office walls and providing employees with the option to work in a tech-free space for a portion of the day. Employees reported increased productivity and decreased fatigue, as they were able to focus more easily without the constant interference of wireless signals.

3. The RF-Free Café in New York City

A café in New York City decided to create an RF-free zone for customers who wanted a peaceful, tech-free environment. The café provided wired connections for customers who needed to work but restricted the use of smartphones and Wi-Fi in certain areas. The response was overwhelmingly positive, with many patrons citing the reduction in digital distractions as a key factor in their decision to spend more time at the café.

Conclusion

Building an RF-free zone in your home or workplace can have profound benefits for your physical health, mental well-being, and overall quality of life. By assessing your environment, implementing shielding solutions, and replacing wireless technologies with wired alternatives, you can create spaces that foster relaxation, focus, and meaningful human connection. Whether it's for sleep, work, or relaxation, an RF-free zone can help reduce stress, improve cognitive function, and provide a much-needed break from the constant exposure to RF radiation.

Chapter 20: Preparing for a Low-RF Future

As society continues to advance technologically, the reliance on radio frequency (RF) communication systems seems inevitable. From smartphones and Wi-Fi to Bluetooth and 5G networks, RF waves have become integral to modern life. However, increasing concerns about RF exposure—on both a health and environmental level—have sparked interest in reducing reliance on RF technologies. In this chapter, we will explore how society is preparing for a future with reduced RF communication, the potential benefits of a low-RF environment, and alternatives to traditional RF technologies that could shape the future of communication infrastructure.

How Society is Moving Toward Reduced RF Reliance

Over the past few decades, RF communication has revolutionized the way we interact, work, and entertain ourselves. However, as we become more aware of the health, privacy, and security risks associated with RF exposure, there has been a push to reduce dependency on these technologies.

1. The Role of 5G and the Push for More Efficient Technology

One of the most significant technological advancements in recent years is the rollout of 5G networks, which promise faster data speeds, greater connectivity, and more efficient wireless communication. While 5G brings many benefits, it has also raised concerns about increased RF radiation due to the higher frequency signals and more dense network of antennas.

As a response to these concerns, some cities and communities are implementing low-5G solutions. These involve lowering the intensity of RF signals and ensuring that devices only transmit when necessary, helping to minimize exposure without sacrificing the efficiency and benefits of the technology.

2. The Growth of Wired Technology

In parallel with the expansion of wireless technologies, there is a resurgence of interest in wired technologies. While wireless technologies like Wi-Fi, Bluetooth, and cellular data offer convenience, they also contribute to RF exposure. As more people become aware of these risks, there has been a noticeable shift back toward wired alternatives, particularly in environments where high-speed communication and data integrity are critical.

- **Ethernet networks** in homes and businesses are being upgraded to offer faster, more stable connections without the RF emissions associated with Wi-Fi.
- **Wired charging stations** are becoming more common in workspaces and public areas, reducing reliance on wireless charging pads, which emit RF radiation.
- **Landline phones**, though less common, are still in use in some households and businesses as a safer alternative to mobile phones.

By embracing wired communication where possible, society can reduce overall RF exposure while still benefiting from advanced technological solutions.

The Potential for a Future with Minimal RF Communication

A future with minimal RF communication is not just about reducing exposure to harmful radiation, but also about adopting alternative technologies that prioritize sustainability, privacy, and health.

1. The Shift Toward Low-Energy Technologies

Low-energy communication technologies, such as **Li-Fi** (Light Fidelity), are emerging as potential alternatives to traditional RF-based communication. Li-Fi uses light to transmit data, offering the same capabilities as Wi-Fi but without the need for RF waves. By utilizing visible light, Li-Fi can provide ultra-fast communication without contributing to RF exposure.

The potential of Li-Fi

2. Decentralized Communication Systems

Another innovative shift on the horizon is the rise of decentralized communication systems that rely less on centralized RF towers and more on direct communication between devices. These technologies can use low-power, short-range wireless communication protocols, such as **Bluetooth Low Energy (BLE)** and **mesh networks**, to create more localized and private communication channels.

Mesh networks

3. The Role of Quantum Communication

Quantum communication is still in its early stages, but it holds tremendous promise for the future of wireless communication. Quantum systems rely on the principles of quantum mechanics to encrypt and transmit data in ways that are theoretically immune to eavesdropping or interception. These systems could function with minimal RF exposure and could be much more secure than current wireless technologies.

Quantum key distribution (QKD)

Exploring Alternatives to RF Technologies

While it is unlikely that RF-based technologies will disappear entirely in the near future, there is a growing movement to explore alternatives that prioritize sustainability and health.

1. Energy Harvesting and Autonomous Systems

Emerging technologies are exploring the possibility of using alternative power sources to reduce the need for RF-powered systems. **Energy harvesting**, such as capturing solar or kinetic energy, could power communication devices without the need for RF radiation. Additionally, **autonomous systems** like drones and robots could rely on non-RF communication methods, such as infrared, to communicate with one another.

These advancements could lead to a future where communication devices no longer require RF signals to function, drastically reducing the environmental and health impacts associated with wireless communication.

2. RF-Independent Smart Cities

Smart cities are evolving to incorporate RF-free solutions for communication, energy management, and transportation. While traditional smart city infrastructure relies heavily on RF-based communication systems, innovations are being made to integrate alternative methods of communication into urban environments.

Underground communication networks

optical fiber networks

Preparing for Changes in Communication Infrastructure

The future of RF communication will likely involve a combination of both RF-based and non-RF technologies. Preparing for this future requires adaptation from governments, businesses, and individuals alike. Governments will need to establish regulations and standards that promote the safe and responsible use of RF technologies while encouraging the development of alternatives.

1. Government Regulations and Infrastructure Development

As RF technologies evolve, governments will play a crucial role in regulating their use and promoting innovation in alternative communication technologies. Policymakers will need to focus on:

- Establishing limits on RF exposure levels.
- Encouraging research into RF-free alternatives and supporting the development of sustainable infrastructure.
- Collaborating with tech companies to ensure that new communication systems prioritize environmental and health concerns.

2. Public Awareness and Education

The shift toward low-RF technologies will require a concerted effort in public education. Individuals must be informed about the potential risks of RF exposure and the benefits of reducing their reliance on wireless communication. This includes promoting the use of safer alternatives and encouraging people to adopt practices that reduce RF exposure in their daily lives.

Educational campaigns

Conclusion

Preparing for a low-RF future involves embracing alternative technologies that reduce RF exposure while still allowing for efficient communication. With innovations like Li-Fi, mesh networks, and quantum communication on the horizon, we are moving toward a more sustainable and health-conscious approach to communication. By transitioning to wired solutions, decentralizing communication systems, and encouraging smarter infrastructure choices, society can reduce its reliance on RF technologies while improving privacy, safety, and overall well-being. The path toward a low-RF future is an exciting one, offering the promise of healthier, safer, and more secure communication solutions for all.

Chapter 21: Challenges in RF Blocking

The growing awareness of the potential health risks associated with radio frequency (RF) exposure has led many individuals to seek ways to block or reduce RF radiation. While RF blocking is an effective approach to minimizing exposure, it comes with its own set of challenges. In this chapter, we will explore the technical, economic, and social hurdles that individuals and organizations face when attempting to block RF waves. We will also discuss the trade-offs between RF shielding and modern conveniences, how to strike a balance between shielding and maintaining connectivity, and how to address the skepticism and resistance that often accompanies RF-blocking solutions.

Technical Challenges

Blocking RF signals may seem like a simple task on the surface, but achieving effective and consistent shielding presents a range of technical challenges.

1. Effective Shielding Materials

Choosing the right materials for RF shielding can be challenging, as different materials have varying effectiveness at blocking different frequencies of RF waves. While metals like copper and aluminum are commonly used in RF shielding, other materials, such as conductive fabrics or special paints, may be less effective or more difficult to work with.

- **Challenges with Conductive Fabrics**: Conductive fabrics, which are often used in DIY RF-blocking solutions, can be expensive and difficult to install. While they are effective at blocking RF signals, the installation process is not always as straightforward as other shielding materials like metals. Additionally, conductive fabrics may not provide complete shielding, especially in areas with high RF exposure or when used in thin layers.
- **Installation Complexity**: For large spaces such as entire rooms or buildings, installing RF-blocking materials like Faraday cages or conductive paint can be complex and time-consuming. This requires expert knowledge and, in some cases, specialized equipment for precise installation.

2. Signal Penetration

RF signals are not always easy to block due to their ability to penetrate various materials, particularly when those materials are not specifically designed to shield against RF waves. Even in situations where RF-blocking materials are used, signals may still find ways to leak through gaps, seams, and openings.

- **Window Shielding**: Windows are a common point of RF signal penetration. While metallic window films or specialized RF-blocking window treatments can reduce exposure, they may not block all frequencies and may impact the aesthetics of the space. Balancing full RF protection and maintaining natural light or a desirable view is an ongoing challenge.
- **Gaps and Leaks**: Achieving a completely RF-free environment requires a sealed space without any gaps. For example, if a room is shielded with conductive fabric or metal, any holes or openings—such as doors, windows, or electrical outlets—can allow RF signals to leak in. Achieving a truly secure RF-blocked zone requires addressing these gaps effectively.

Economic Challenges

While the benefits of blocking RF exposure are clear, the cost of effective RF shielding can be a significant barrier for many individuals or organizations. Here are some of the economic considerations involved in setting up RF-blocking solutions.

1. Upfront Costs

The initial investment for RF-blocking materials can be expensive, particularly for high-quality shielding solutions. Faraday cages, conductive fabrics, shielding paints, and other advanced materials can all require a substantial financial commitment, especially for larger areas.

- **Faraday Cages and Professional Installations**: For professional-grade RF shielding, Faraday cages or custom-built shielding solutions often require the expertise of trained installers. The cost of these services can add up, making it less accessible for individuals who want to set up RF-free zones at home.
- **RF-blocking Technology for Personal Devices**: Although the growing market for RF-blocking products like phone cases, laptop shields, and wearable tech is making it easier for individuals to protect themselves, the cost of these products can still be a limiting factor for many people. The need for specialized products for each device can add up over time, especially when considering long-term use.

2. Ongoing Maintenance and Upkeep

In addition to the initial cost of setting up an RF-free environment, there is also the issue of maintaining and updating the shielding solutions. Over time, shielding materials can degrade, especially those exposed to wear and tear, humidity, or environmental factors.

- **Longevity of Materials**: The durability of shielding materials like conductive fabrics or paints depends on how well they are maintained. They may require reapplication or replacement over time, adding to the overall cost of the system.
- **System Upgrades**: As RF technologies evolve, so too must our shielding solutions. For example, new cellular communication networks, such as 5G, may require different shielding methods or materials that offer higher frequency protection. Staying up to date with emerging RF technologies may necessitate upgrading current shielding systems, which can be costly.

Social Challenges

Beyond the technical and economic obstacles, there are also social challenges related to blocking RF exposure. These challenges often stem from a broader societal reliance on wireless communication, as well as resistance to change and misconceptions about the risks of RF radiation.

1. Resistance to Change

One of the biggest social challenges to RF blocking is the general reluctance to move away from convenient, modern technologies. Wireless communication has become an essential part of daily life, and many people view it as too difficult or unnecessary to live without.

- **Convenience Over Health**: People often prioritize the convenience and connectivity provided by wireless technologies, such as Wi-Fi, Bluetooth, and mobile phones, over the potential health risks associated with constant RF exposure. The idea of disconnecting from these technologies, especially in the context of work or social interactions, can be perceived as inconvenient or unrealistic.
- **Cultural Norms**: In many cultures, technology and connectivity are seen as essential to personal and professional success. The societal expectation to be constantly connected can lead to resistance to the idea of RF-free zones, especially in workplaces or public spaces. This cultural bias can make it difficult to implement widespread changes in how people interact with technology.

2. Misconceptions About RF Risks

There are still many misconceptions about the health risks associated with RF exposure. The lack of widespread understanding regarding the potential dangers of RF radiation can contribute to the reluctance to block these signals. The scientific debate surrounding RF and health continues to fuel skepticism.

- **Underestimating the Risk**: Many people are unaware of the potential long-term health effects of RF exposure, such as increased risks of cancer, fertility issues, and neurological disorders. The absence of conclusive, universally accepted studies on these risks makes it challenging to build public support for RF blocking initiatives.
- **Misinformation**: Misinformation and confusion about RF and electromagnetic fields (EMF) are rampant, particularly on social media. While there are credible studies indicating the risks of prolonged RF exposure, there are also numerous sources downplaying these concerns. This conflicting information makes it difficult to navigate the decision of whether to invest in RF protection.

Balancing Shielding with Maintaining Connectivity

One of the most significant challenges in RF blocking is finding the balance between minimizing RF exposure and maintaining the convenience and functionality of wireless technologies. While it is possible to block RF signals completely in certain spaces, doing so may interfere with the use of essential devices like mobile phones, Wi-Fi routers, and Bluetooth-enabled devices.

- **Selective Shielding**: Instead of blocking all RF signals, individuals may choose to selectively shield specific areas where they spend the most time, such as bedrooms or home offices. This allows them to maintain connectivity in other parts of their home or workplace while still protecting themselves from excessive RF exposure in high-risk areas.
- **Smart Technology Solutions**: Another option is to use advanced technology to manage RF exposure without completely eliminating it. For instance, devices like Wi-Fi routers with adjustable power settings or timers can allow for control over when and how much RF radiation is emitted, reducing exposure while still enabling connectivity.

Conclusion

While RF blocking offers significant benefits in terms of reducing exposure to harmful radiation, it also comes with a range of technical, economic, and social challenges. Effectively shielding against RF signals requires careful consideration of the materials, costs, and long-term maintenance required to achieve optimal results. Furthermore, the widespread acceptance of wireless technology and the misconceptions surrounding RF risks can make it difficult to motivate change on a larger scale. By addressing these challenges and striving for a balance between connectivity and health, society can move toward safer, more conscious approaches to RF communication.

Chapter 22: RF Blocking for Health and Wellness

In recent years, the awareness surrounding the potential health effects of radio frequency (RF) radiation has surged. As more people become concerned about the impact of prolonged RF exposure, many are looking into RF blocking solutions not just for privacy and security but for the potential health benefits as well. This chapter explores how RF blocking can contribute to overall wellness, the role it plays in improving sleep quality, enhancing productivity, and supporting a healthier lifestyle. It will also provide practical tips for integrating RF-free practices into daily routines to maximize health benefits.

The Role of RF Blocking in Wellness Practices

Wellness has become an integral part of modern life, encompassing physical, mental, and emotional health. One aspect that has gained attention is the role of environmental factors, such as RF radiation, in our well-being. By blocking or reducing RF exposure, many individuals have reported significant improvements in their health, making RF blocking an essential part of their wellness routine.

1. Improved Sleep Quality

One of the most significant benefits of reducing RF exposure is the improvement in sleep quality. RF waves emitted by devices such as smartphones, routers, and microwaves have been linked to disruptions in sleep patterns. The body's circadian rhythms, which regulate the sleep-wake cycle, can be disturbed by constant exposure to RF radiation, leading to difficulties falling asleep, staying asleep, or experiencing restful sleep.

- **Impact on Melatonin Production**: RF radiation can interfere with the production of melatonin, the hormone responsible for regulating sleep. Studies suggest that exposure to RF radiation, especially before bedtime, can suppress melatonin production, making it harder for individuals to fall asleep and experience restorative sleep cycles.
- **Sleep Disorders**: Those who are sensitive to EMF (electromagnetic fields) have reported symptoms like insomnia, fatigue, and restless sleep. RF-blocking practices, such as using shielding devices, placing phones on airplane mode at night, and limiting screen time before bed, can reduce these disturbances and improve overall sleep quality.

2. Reduced Stress and Anxiety

The constant bombardment of RF waves can contribute to heightened stress levels. The presence of wireless communication systems like cell towers, Wi-Fi, and mobile phones can create an environment where the body is in a state of constant low-level stress due to exposure to EMF radiation. By blocking RF radiation, individuals have reported feeling calmer, more relaxed, and less anxious.

- **Electromagnetic Sensitivity**: Some individuals, particularly those with electromagnetic sensitivity (also known as electrohypersensitivity or EHS), experience symptoms such as headaches, irritability, and stress when exposed to RF signals. By taking steps to block or reduce RF exposure, they can often experience a noticeable reduction in these symptoms, leading to lower stress and anxiety levels.
- **Digital Detox**: A growing trend of digital detoxing has been gaining popularity, where people intentionally disconnect from digital devices and reduce their exposure to RF radiation. This practice not only helps with reducing RF-related stress but also provides psychological benefits, such as greater mindfulness and a sense of relaxation.

How RF Protection Impacts Productivity

Reducing RF exposure can also have a profound effect on productivity, particularly in work environments where individuals are surrounded by wireless technology. RF radiation has been associated with several cognitive impacts, including impaired concentration, memory difficulties, and brain fog. By implementing RF-blocking strategies, individuals can improve their focus and mental clarity, thus enhancing their productivity.

1. Cognitive Function and Focus

Excessive RF radiation can negatively impact cognitive function, making it harder to concentrate or perform tasks that require mental focus. Studies have suggested that long-term exposure to RF waves could alter brain activity and impair memory processes, leading to reduced performance in both academic and professional settings.

- **Mental Fatigue**: Continuous exposure to RF radiation, especially from close-range devices like smartphones or laptops, can contribute to mental fatigue. By limiting RF exposure in workspaces—such as using shielded devices or limiting wireless communication—individuals may experience an increase in cognitive function and improved ability to concentrate.
- **Increased Energy Levels**: People who reduce their RF exposure through blocking or shielding techniques report increased energy levels and improved productivity. When the body is not constantly dealing with the strain of processing external RF signals, it can focus on mental tasks without the added interference.

2. Reduced Headaches and Eye Strain

RF exposure, particularly from screens, can lead to headaches and eye strain, making it difficult to work for long hours without discomfort. Blocking or reducing RF radiation can significantly reduce these issues, allowing for more efficient and comfortable work experiences.

- **Headache Relief**: Many individuals who experience frequent headaches due to RF exposure have reported improvements by using RF-blocking phone cases, wearable shielding devices, or turning off Wi-Fi signals during work hours. Reducing RF-related strain on the body leads to fewer headaches and better overall health.
- **Eye Protection**: Prolonged exposure to screen-based devices, which emit RF waves, can contribute to digital eye strain. Implementing shielding solutions to block radiation from screens, particularly in environments with multiple devices, can reduce the risk of developing eye discomfort or long-term vision problems.

Integrating RF-Free Practices into Daily Routines

For those looking to incorporate RF-free practices into their daily routines, there are a variety of strategies to choose from. From simple lifestyle changes to more advanced shielding solutions, these practices can help create a healthier, more balanced environment free from excess RF radiation.

1. Lifestyle Changes for Minimizing Exposure

- **Turn Off Devices**: One of the simplest ways to reduce RF exposure is to turn off devices when not in use. This includes switching off Wi-Fi routers, turning phones to airplane mode, or disconnecting Bluetooth devices during sleep or work.

- **Use Wired Connections**: Opt for wired connections for internet, phones, and other communication devices rather than relying on Wi-Fi or Bluetooth. This reduces exposure to electromagnetic fields generated by wireless communication technologies.

- **RF-blocking Wearables**: There is a growing market for wearable RF-blocking devices, including clothing and accessories that incorporate shielding materials. These can help reduce exposure to radiation during everyday activities such as commuting or shopping.

2. Creating RF-free Zones at Home and Work

- **Designating Tech-Free Zones**: Dedicate specific areas in your home or office to be RF-free zones. These areas can be used for rest, relaxation, or concentration, free from the constant buzz of electronic devices. Use shielding materials such as Faraday bags for personal items or RF-blocking paint for rooms that need complete isolation.
- **Smart Home Adjustments**: With the rise of smart homes, many devices are connected via wireless signals. While convenience is key, consider limiting the number of smart devices or opting for models that do not rely on Wi-Fi or Bluetooth. If possible, install RF-blocking window films or use curtains to shield against external signals.

Conclusion

RF blocking is not just about protecting yourself from potential health risks; it is also about enhancing your overall wellness. By reducing RF exposure, individuals can experience improved sleep, reduced stress, enhanced focus, and better productivity. As we continue to learn more about the long-term impacts of RF radiation on health, incorporating RF-free practices into daily routines will become increasingly essential for maintaining a balanced and healthy lifestyle. From lifestyle changes to advanced shielding solutions, blocking RF radiation provides an effective way to take control of your health and well-being in an increasingly connected world.

Chapter 23: RF Blocking and the Future of Communication

The future of communication is being shaped by advancements in technology, some of which promise to radically change the way we interact with the world. Radio Frequency (RF) communication has been the backbone of modern wireless technology, powering everything from smartphones to Wi-Fi networks to global satellite communication. However, as concerns over RF exposure, privacy, and security continue to grow, RF blocking technologies are increasingly becoming a vital part of the conversation. In this chapter, we will explore how RF blocking may influence the future of communication, the potential shifts in how we use wireless technologies, and emerging technologies that could render RF communication less necessary. The promise of safer communication solutions is on the horizon, and this chapter will provide insight into these emerging trends.

How RF Blocking Could Influence the Future of Communication

As wireless technologies have become more integrated into our daily lives, the demand for protection against RF radiation has also increased. RF blocking solutions are not just a response to health concerns but also play a key role in safeguarding privacy and security. The increasing adoption of RF blocking could impact the communication landscape in several ways:

1. Privacy and Security Enhancements

In a world where data breaches, hacking, and surveillance are persistent threats, RF blocking solutions could become more integral in protecting personal privacy. With the rise of IoT (Internet of Things) devices, more data is being transmitted wirelessly than ever before, and that data is vulnerable to interception. RF blocking technology, such as Faraday cages and signal-blocking materials, could help protect sensitive data from being intercepted by malicious actors or unwanted surveillance.

As we see more sophisticated RF-based hacking techniques, including signal jamming and spoofing, RF blocking tools could become critical for securing communication networks and preventing unauthorized access to personal and corporate data.

2. Enhanced Health Protection

With concerns about the health effects of prolonged RF exposure, including potential links to cancer, neurological issues, and reproductive health, RF blocking technologies could become essential for creating safer environments in homes, workplaces, and public spaces. Future advancements in shielding materials could provide more effective and less intrusive methods to block harmful radiation without compromising connectivity.

As research into the health impacts of RF radiation continues, regulations may evolve, making it necessary for organizations to adopt RF protection measures in certain environments, particularly in workplaces where workers are exposed to high levels of RF radiation.

3. Integration with Smart Cities

The rise of smart cities, which rely heavily on wireless communication networks to monitor traffic, manage energy use, and provide public services, presents new challenges. These environments could benefit from widespread RF blocking solutions that provide localized protection for residents and businesses while allowing public infrastructure to operate efficiently.

As the balance between connectivity and privacy/security becomes more important, RF blocking could become an essential feature of smart cities, ensuring that personal data is protected while still allowing cities to thrive on wireless communication systems.

Potential Shifts in How We Use Wireless Technologies

While RF blocking is an important step in protecting individuals from the adverse effects of RF radiation, the very nature of wireless communication technology is evolving. The future of communication will likely see a shift toward alternative technologies that require less reliance on traditional RF signals. These changes could shape how we use wireless communication systems in the years to come.

1. 5G and Beyond: Opportunities and Challenges

5G technology promises faster speeds, lower latency, and more reliable connections, enabling everything from autonomous vehicles to remote healthcare services. However, 5G's widespread use will result in more RF radiation, as new frequencies are utilized to support the network. As concerns about RF exposure continue to grow, innovative RF shielding solutions could be integrated into 5G networks to provide protection for sensitive individuals and vulnerable areas.

The future may also see the development of 6G, which could introduce even more advanced communication methods, such as terahertz waves, which have higher frequencies and shorter wavelengths than current RF technologies. As we transition to these new communication protocols, RF blocking technologies will need to evolve to address the challenges posed by higher-frequency radiation.

2. Wireless Power Transmission: Reducing RF Exposure

Wireless power transmission is another exciting frontier that promises to revolutionize how we power devices. By using RF waves to transmit power, wireless charging stations could eliminate the need for physical connections between devices and their charging units. However, these systems also introduce new RF exposure risks. RF blocking technologies will play a role in mitigating potential health risks associated with these new methods of power transfer.

Moreover, advances in wireless power transmission could lead to solutions that make it easier to shield areas where high-powered RF signals are in use, ensuring that these technologies are deployed safely.

3. The Rise of Quantum Communication

Quantum communication is a cutting-edge technology that relies on the principles of quantum mechanics to create secure communication channels that are virtually immune to hacking. This revolutionary technology could eventually replace traditional RF-based communication systems in certain high-security applications, providing a new way to communicate without the risk of interception.

While quantum communication may still be in its early stages, its promise for the future of secure communication could render traditional RF blocking measures less important in highly sensitive areas. However, until quantum technologies become more widespread, RF blocking will remain a crucial component of safeguarding data and communication.

New Technologies That May Render RF Less Necessary

The development of new communication technologies may reduce our dependence on traditional RF-based systems. These innovations could lead to more efficient, safer, and less intrusive ways to communicate.

1. Li-Fi (Light Fidelity)

Li-Fi is an emerging wireless communication technology that uses light waves instead of RF signals to transmit data. This technology operates in the visible light spectrum, which is considered safer than RF radiation. Li-Fi offers the potential for faster data transfer speeds and greater energy efficiency. As Li-Fi technology continues to develop, it could gradually replace Wi-Fi in certain applications, reducing the need for RF radiation.

Incorporating Li-Fi into homes, offices, and public spaces could significantly reduce RF exposure while still enabling seamless, high-speed communication. This shift could lead to a future where RF-blocking solutions become less necessary in environments where Li-Fi is the primary method of wireless communication.

2. Tactile Communication

Another exciting development is the exploration of tactile communication systems that use vibrations or touch to convey information. These systems could potentially eliminate the need for RF waves in certain communication applications, especially in settings where privacy and security are paramount, such as in military or healthcare environments. Tactile communication could also be used in consumer technology, providing an alternative to traditional wireless communication methods.

As these technologies evolve, RF blocking may shift from being primarily focused on health concerns to addressing privacy and security needs in increasingly connected environments.

The Promise of Safer Communication Solutions

As technology continues to advance, the future of communication will likely see a combination of RF blocking solutions and emerging technologies that aim to provide faster, more secure, and less harmful communication methods. Innovations like Li-Fi, quantum communication, and tactile communication hold the potential to reduce our dependence on traditional RF-based systems, making the need for blocking solutions less pressing in some areas.

However, until these technologies become mainstream, RF blocking will continue to play a crucial role in protecting our health, privacy, and security. By continuing to develop more effective shielding materials, embracing new communication technologies, and remaining vigilant about the risks of RF exposure, we can ensure that the future of communication is safer and more sustainable for everyone.

Conclusion

The future of communication is undoubtedly exciting, with advancements that promise faster, more secure, and more efficient ways to connect with one another. As RF technologies evolve and new alternatives emerge, the importance of RF blocking will shift and adapt. While some of these changes may reduce our reliance on RF communication, the need for protective measures will continue to play a key role in ensuring that communication remains safe, private, and secure. The promise of a safer communication future lies in the continued development of RF blocking technologies, new communication methods, and a commitment to balancing connectivity with health and security.

Chapter 24: Myths and Misconceptions about RF Waves

As with any complex and evolving topic, radio frequency (RF) waves are subject to misunderstanding, misinformation, and myths. While RF technology is vital to modern communication, the controversy surrounding its potential health risks, privacy concerns, and technological impacts often leads to confusion. In this chapter, we will address the most common myths and misconceptions about RF waves, providing clarity by separating fact from fiction and addressing the misinformation that frequently circulates in the media. By understanding the truth behind these myths, we can make more informed decisions about RF exposure and protection.

Myth 1: RF Waves Are the Same as Ionizing Radiation

One of the most pervasive misconceptions about RF waves is that they are akin to ionizing radiation, like X-rays or ultraviolet rays, which can cause cancer and other health issues by directly altering cellular DNA. This myth has contributed to widespread fear about RF exposure.

Fact: RF waves are non-ionizing radiation, meaning they do not have enough energy to ionize atoms or molecules or remove tightly bound electrons. Unlike ionizing radiation, which can directly damage cellular DNA, non-ionizing radiation primarily causes heating effects. RF waves can raise the temperature of tissue, but they do not cause genetic mutations that lead to cancer in the way that ionizing radiation does. The key difference is the energy level—ionizing radiation has high energy capable of altering atomic structures, while RF waves do not.

Myth 2: RF Exposure Causes Cancer

The link between RF exposure and cancer is one of the most widely discussed topics, and many believe that regular exposure to RF radiation, particularly from devices like cell phones, increases the risk of cancer. Various claims and studies have fueled this fear, with sensational headlines often exaggerating the results of research.

Fact: To date, the overwhelming body of scientific evidence does not support a direct link between RF exposure and cancer. The World Health Organization (WHO), the U.S. National Cancer Institute, and other leading health organizations have found no conclusive evidence that RF radiation from everyday devices like cell phones, Wi-Fi routers, and Bluetooth devices causes cancer. The International Agency for Research on Cancer (IARC) classified RF radiation as possibly carcinogenic (Group 2B) based on some studies, but this does not imply a direct cause-and-effect relationship. The risks remain unproven, and more research is needed.

Myth 3: RF Radiation is Dangerous Only in High Doses

A common belief is that RF radiation is only harmful when it exceeds certain levels, often associated with industrial or scientific environments. Many assume that everyday exposure to devices like smartphones and Wi-Fi routers is safe, as it is well below these "dangerous" levels.

Fact: While it is true that high levels of RF exposure—such as those encountered in specialized environments or from powerful transmission equipment—can pose health risks, the levels emitted by consumer electronics like cell phones, laptops, and household Wi-Fi routers are much lower than the thresholds established by safety standards. These devices operate within safe limits established by regulatory bodies such as the Federal Communications Commission (FCC) and the World Health Organization (WHO). Nevertheless, concerns about potential long-term effects of prolonged exposure at lower levels remain, and research continues into how cumulative, low-level RF exposure may affect health over time.

Myth 4: RF Shielding Completely Eliminates Health Risks

With the growing availability of RF-blocking products—such as phone cases, blankets, and clothing—many people believe that using these shields will entirely eliminate the health risks associated with RF exposure. As a result, there is a sense of security that these products provide full protection from RF radiation.

Fact: While RF shielding can reduce exposure to RF waves, it is important to understand that no shielding product can guarantee complete protection in every situation. The effectiveness of shielding depends on factors such as the type of material used, the frequency of the RF waves, and how well the shielding is applied. In some cases, shielding may be only partially effective, especially in areas where RF signals are pervasive, such as in urban environments with strong mobile networks. Shielding should be seen as part of an overall strategy to manage RF exposure, but it should not be relied on as a sole solution for preventing health risks.

Myth 5: RF Blocking Products Are Unnecessary and Overhyped

On the other side of the spectrum, some people believe that the concern over RF radiation is overstated and that RF-blocking products are merely a marketing ploy aimed at selling unnecessary gadgets. The argument often hinges on the belief that RF radiation levels from everyday devices are so low that no blocking measures are needed.

Fact: While the overall risks of RF radiation exposure remain uncertain, growing evidence suggests that reducing exposure—particularly for vulnerable populations like children, the elderly, and pregnant women—may be beneficial. While RF-blocking products may not be required for everyone, they can offer peace of mind for those who are concerned about long-term exposure or those who work in environments with higher RF levels. Furthermore, as the proliferation of wireless devices continues and 5G networks are rolled out, the need for managing RF exposure may increase. For some individuals, RF-blocking products represent a proactive approach to minimizing exposure in the absence of conclusive long-term studies.

Myth 6: Smart Meters and Wireless Networks Are the Primary RF Threats

With the increased deployment of smart meters and the expansion of wireless networks like 5G, many people have become concerned that these technologies are the primary source of dangerous RF radiation. This fear often stems from the perceived intensity of signals emitted by these systems, especially in the context of 5G's higher frequency bands.

Fact: While it is true that 5G and smart meters use RF radiation, their power levels are still relatively low compared to the levels used in industrial and medical applications. Smart meters, for example, typically emit RF signals for short bursts, and the power levels are far lower than what would be required to cause harm. The key issue is not just the power but the cumulative effect of long-term exposure to RF radiation from all sources—cell phones, Wi-Fi, Bluetooth, smart meters, and others. Regulatory bodies continue to monitor RF safety, and while 5G may introduce higher frequencies, studies have not demonstrated a direct link to adverse health outcomes.

Myth 7: EMF (Electromagnetic Field) Radiation Is Always Harmful

Many people confuse RF radiation with EMF (electromagnetic field) radiation, and some claim that all EMF exposure is harmful. The term "EMF" can refer to a wide range of radiation types, including both ionizing and non-ionizing radiation.

Fact: EMF radiation covers a broad spectrum of energies, and while ionizing EMF (such as X-rays and gamma rays) can be harmful, non-ionizing EMF—such as RF waves—has not been shown to cause the same kind of damage. RF radiation is non-ionizing, meaning it does not have the energy to break molecular bonds or cause the kind of direct DNA damage that ionizing radiation can cause. The potential risks of EMF from RF radiation are still being studied, but current evidence does not support the idea that everyday RF exposure is inherently harmful.

Conclusion

The myths and misconceptions surrounding RF radiation can lead to unnecessary fear, confusion, and poor decision-making. By separating fact from fiction, we can take a more balanced and informed approach to managing RF exposure. While it is important to acknowledge the potential health risks associated with RF radiation, it is equally important to recognize that current scientific evidence does not support the most alarming claims. As our understanding of RF waves continues to evolve, it is essential to stay informed and apply critical thinking when evaluating the various products and solutions aimed at mitigating RF exposure.

Chapter 25: Conclusion

As we reach the end of this guide on mastering the art of disconnecting from radio frequency (RF) waves, it is crucial to reflect on the key themes and ideas we've explored throughout the book. Understanding RF waves and their potential health, privacy, and security risks has empowered us to make more informed decisions about managing our exposure. From shielding technologies to practical, everyday strategies for reducing RF radiation, we've learned the importance of taking control of our environment in an increasingly RF-saturated world. This chapter serves as a recap of our journey and a call to action for integrating RF protection into our lives for a safer, healthier, and more connected future.

The Importance of RF Wave Management

RF waves, a cornerstone of modern communication systems, have undeniably revolutionized how we connect, work, and live. However, with their pervasive nature and potential health concerns, it is essential to approach RF exposure with a balanced perspective. While the scientific community has not definitively established all the long-term risks of RF radiation, it is prudent to take proactive steps to limit unnecessary exposure—particularly as wireless technology continues to evolve.

We've examined the various ways RF exposure can affect our health, with specific focus on the potential risks it poses to sensitive populations such as children, the elderly, and individuals with pre-existing conditions. Although the direct link between RF radiation and conditions like cancer remains inconclusive, scientific studies continue to explore the cumulative impact of exposure from multiple sources.

The Future of RF Blocking and Communication

The future of RF blocking technology holds promise, with ongoing advancements in materials science and engineering. Emerging innovations such as more effective shielding materials, RF-blocking fabrics, and portable devices that help mitigate exposure are reshaping the landscape of personal and environmental protection. Moreover, advancements in AI and machine learning are creating new opportunities for real-time RF wave monitoring and more intelligent, adaptive shielding solutions.

As society moves toward the rollout of next-generation wireless technologies like 5G, the importance of developing sustainable and effective RF blocking solutions becomes even more critical. While these technologies promise faster communication speeds and more efficient systems, they also raise new concerns about increased exposure to higher-frequency RF radiation. Preparing for a future that minimizes unnecessary exposure while embracing technological advances will be crucial for maintaining both the convenience and safety of wireless communications.

Integrating RF Protection into Your Life

Throughout this book, we have explored practical strategies for integrating RF protection into your personal and professional life. Whether it's creating an RF-free zone at home, using RF-blocking accessories for personal devices, or understanding the legal and ethical implications of RF shielding, the goal has been to offer a comprehensive toolkit to help you manage your exposure.

The journey toward minimizing RF exposure does not require drastic measures, but rather a series of thoughtful and intentional steps. Simple adjustments, such as turning off Wi-Fi routers at night, using speakerphone instead of holding a cell phone to your ear, and utilizing RF-blocking cases for devices, can make a significant difference in the amount of RF radiation you are exposed to on a daily basis.

Additionally, the growing awareness around RF radiation is paving the way for broader societal shifts. As more people begin to prioritize their health and wellness by reducing RF exposure, we may see the creation of more RF-safe environments, both in private spaces and public institutions. Incorporating RF-blocking technologies into new buildings, offices, and schools could eventually become a standard practice, ensuring that we strike a balance between embracing connectivity and safeguarding our health.

A Call to Action

It is clear that the future of communication and technology will be shaped by our collective approach to managing RF radiation. As individuals, we have the power to make choices that protect our health and well-being. Whether you choose to implement shielding materials in your home, use RF-blocking accessories, or simply become more aware of your exposure to RF waves, every step you take contributes to creating a safer environment for yourself and others.

As a society, it's important to continue questioning the status quo and pushing for regulations and standards that prioritize health while still embracing technological innovation. Governments, scientists, and industry leaders must work together to better understand the long-term effects of RF exposure and create policies that protect public health without stifling progress.

This is a call to action for a healthier, more connected future. By mastering the art of disconnecting from unnecessary RF exposure, we can lead by example and inspire others to take control of their environment. The key to a safe and prosperous future lies in our ability to adapt and protect ourselves while continuing to benefit from the vast advancements in wireless communication.

The journey to mastering RF protection is one of awareness, balance, and proactive action. The tools and strategies provided in this book offer the foundation for creating a world where health, safety, and connectivity coexist harmoniously. Let us move forward with a commitment to creating a safer, healthier, and more sustainable future—one where the benefits of technology are maximized, and the risks are minimized.

Final Thoughts

As we conclude this guide, it is essential to recognize that the management of RF exposure is not a one-time task, but a continual process. By staying informed, monitoring our environment, and embracing technologies that reduce RF exposure, we can make educated decisions that benefit our health, privacy, and security in the long term. By making small but impactful changes in our everyday lives, we can contribute to a world where safe and responsible RF use is the norm.

In a rapidly advancing world, taking the time to prioritize safety and well-being should be a key part of embracing new technologies. Ultimately, it's about finding the right balance between convenience and protection, ensuring that the future of communication remains both innovative and safe.

Now, armed with the knowledge and tools to manage RF waves, it's time to embrace the power of informed decision-making and step into a future where we can thrive both in our connected world and in the protection of our health.

www.ingramcontent.com/pod-product-compliance
Lightning Source LLC
Chambersburg PA
CBHW082246220526
45469CB00009B/2888